PREDICTABLY DISASTROUS RESULTS

Laurie Notaro

Oraton Press
Eugene, Oregon

Predictably Disastrous Results:
Vintage Legends Volume II

Laurie Notaro

Copyright 2016 by Laurie Notaro

All rights reserved under International
and Pan-American Copyright Conventions.

Published in the United States by Oraton Press

No part of this work may be distributed, republished,
copied or sold without the express permission
of the author and Oraton Press.

A Note to Very Discerning Readers:

Please be aware, before starting this book, that there will be typos. There will probably be a lot of typos. I even toyed with the idea of calling this book "There Will Be Typos," but my mother said it was stupid and that no one would buy a book called that. However, if a typo is cause enough for you to not enjoy this book and then leave a nasty review on Amazon asking if my editor died, you may want to ask for a refund at this very moment. I am a writer, a shitty typist, and am horrible at copy editing, although I do try. I give it my best. But much like I cannot afford a gardener to make my yard perfect, I have no budget for the expertise required for some readers. Therefore, my lawn has brown spots where dogs have peed and I was very proud of a tall plant with yellow flowers that everyone else knew was a weed but me. This book is a lot like that.

The majority of this book was written before the mass invasion of cell phones, iPads, Roku, FitBits and Tivo. If slipping for a moment into a world where I refer to a landline, a television lacking a remote, or a typewriter, will upset you, you may not want to go any further. It may be a frightening and primitive place for those born after 1990.

I'll think of some other disclaimers as I go along, but for now, I leave you with this warning. If you get a glass of wine or an Ativan, you and I can have a good time. I promise. Enjoy this book for what it is, a trip back in time. This is a labor of love project; I did it myself, late at night, on weekends or in the early morning. I did it because I thought it would be fun to get this stuff out and circulating again. But know that I am a horribly imperfect human being. So kindly forgive mistakes, foibles and errors.

Most of this book takes place in the century before ours. It was a time when phones were still attached to walls, you wrote checks at the grocery store, and you ruled if you had a cassette deck in your car. Embrace the era in this little time-capsule.

Awesomely,
Laurie

That's Alarming

It could have happened to anybody whose husband came home a little late from happy hour and tried to set the burglar alarm for the night.

The siren was blasting; the dog was barking. The phone started to ring shrilly, and in 15 seconds, our peaceful little house had been transformed into a commercial for Valium. My husband was stationed in front of the burglar alarm, desperately trying to punch in numbers to turn it off.

"Did you eat bread before you went to happy hour?" I shouted. "You know you can't go to happy hour on an empty stomach! The last time you came home like this, you were determined to write an off-Broadway production based on the Foreigner 'Four' album!"

"You said it was okay because we had a designated driver!" he shouted from the laundry room. "And that play would have totally worked! I AM the Dirty White Boy!"

The phone kept screaming as I ran from the bathroom to answer it. I was getting ready for bed when calamity erupted, and sprinted to the phone as quickly as I could, dodging our dog who consistently kept trying to leap into my arms.

"This is the security company calling," the voice on the other end said. "Your alarm is on."

"I know, I'm sorry," I replied. "My husband can't shut it off! Get off my back, would you!"

"Pardon me?" the security lady said.

"I'm sorry," I hastily answered. "I'm talking to my dog!"

"Is this a false alarm?" she asked.

"Yes," I told her. "Leave me alone!"

"Ma'am?"

"Sorry," I said. "My dog. Everything's fine, really!"

BANG! our front door shook. BANG! BANG! BANG!

"I need your security code, please," the lady said.

"Um," I said, trying to think. "It's my nephew's birthday! Wait, it's our anniversary! No, I think it's my body fat ratio!"

BANG! BANG! BANG! The front door shook again, as my dog whined and scrambled to hide under the coffee table.

Hang on, I said, putting down the phone to answer the door.

"POLICE!! OPEN UP!!" I heard from the other side.

I opened the door and saw two uniformed officers on my porch.

"Everything's fine," I told them. "My husband tried to set the alarm on an empty stomach."

"We need to see some ID," the first policeman said, looking at me curiously.

"AHH!" my husband screamed from the back of the house. "I'm going to KILL this thing! I'm gonna tear you apart with my bare hands!"

I smiled quickly. "He's talking to the alarm," I said nonchalantly.

"I HATE YOU! I HATE YOU! I HATE YOU!" my husband yelled.

"Honey," I yelled, running into the kitchen. "The police are here! Shut up!"

"You're kidding!" he said in shock. "Are we on COPS? They don't have cameras, do they?"

"WHAT?" I said, getting frustrated. "No, we're not on COPS!"

"Good," he replied. "You're not wearing a bra under your shirt!"

"Big deal," I said, getting more flustered.

"Or pants!" he added.

"Just how much did you drink?" I asked before I looked down and gasped. No pants. Only underwear, of the brief style, that had turned a dingy kind of gray when I had washed them with new black tights, and, thankfully, a rather long T-shirt. I'm married. I chew with my mouth open. I don't close the door when I go to the bathroom. I stopped shaving the day after my wedding. What do I need fancy underwear for? There's no one left to impress.

"Give me your shorts!" I demanded, pointing to my husband's boxers. Then I'll be naked!

"Ma'am," the police man called from the living room. "I need to see some ID!"

"You are so selfish!" I hissed to my husband. "I have an Emotional Injury Journal from the Oprah show and I am going to write this down in it, you know!"

"You're injured, ma'am?" the policeman called. "Do you want us to call an ambulance?"

I pulled my T-shirt down as far as I could and went back into the living room.

"No," I replied. "I'm going back into therapy tomorrow."

I flipped through my wallet and found my driver's license, and, miraculously, the security code written on a card. I picked up the phone, still resting patiently on the kitchen table.

"I'm sorry," I said to the security lady. "The code isn't my nephew's birthday. It's my husband's blood alcohol level."

I handed my ID to the policeman, who was now standing in the living room.

"He should have eaten some bread," the lady replied. "Make sure you note this in your Oprah journal."

"Pen is in hand, sister," I replied before I hung up.

Mercifully, the alarm stopped screaming. The cop handed back my license.

You look much different in that picture, he mentioned.

"Well, it was a long time ago," I said wearily. "I wore make-up, practiced hygiene and had fancy underwear then."

"And probably pants," he added, smirking. "Expect to get a letter from the Police Department in a couple of weeks."

"Because of the pants?" I asked.

"For the false alarm," he informed me as he turned and walked out the door with a look that said, "What is it with these women? They get a ring, a handful of empty promises and then throw away all of their razors?"

"I shaved off enough body hair before I got married to carpet my whole house!" I called after them. "I deserve this!"

I saw my husband secretly trying to creep into the bedroom.

"Hey, Mr. Magoo!" I called. "From now on, if you go to happy hour, you are not allowed to touch anything when you come home that blinks or is plugged in!"

"Are we in trouble?" he mumbled.

"I don't know yet," I answered. "They're going to send us a letter."

"Urgent! Urgent!" I heard my husband hum as he began to struggle with another electric appliance. "Emergency! Wait and see how urgent our love can be... It's urgent urgent urgent urgent urgent....."

"I'll set the alarm clock, Juke Box Hero," I offered.

YOUR KISSES ARE YUCKY

I always thought I was a pro at handling rejection.

At least that's what the engraving says on the Loser Championship Cup that proudly rests on the mantle of my fireplace.

As a teenager, I had four boyfriends that turned out to be gay, two of whom eventually dated each other.

I have enough "Thanks for asking, but you suck" letters from book publishers to wallpaper my office with, at that's above and beyond the ones my agent sends me in a crisp brown envelope every week.

So you understand why I thought I had seen it all, had touched and been singed by the flames of multiple humiliations and have lived to tell the tales.

It turns out I didn't know anything.

I didn't know the first thing about heartbreak until the moment, two weeks ago, that I saw my three-year old nephew Nicholas wipe my kiss from his mouth with the back of his dimpled baby hand.

At first I had the ego to laugh. "Did I tickle you?" I asked him as he looked at me from his car seat in my sister's minivan.

"NO," he declared.

"Then why did you just do that?" I inquired.

He took a deep breath, rolled his eyes and said plainly, "Your kisses are YUCKY."

Now naturally, I've heard that before from one of those aforementioned boyfriends that considered the affections of someone named Alan far more delightful. But this time, coming from my nephew, it really hurt.

My nephew is supposed to be my little pal. I'm the Good Time Aunt; I bring him a toy every time I see him to bribe his love. I know that works, because when I was a little, both my Auntie Ida and my Uncle Jimmy used to bring me toys every single time they came to visit. On one occasion, I got so excited to see them that I fell down a whole flight of stairs, punched out my eye and very nearly alleviated the need for future orthodontic work by smacking my two tiny buck teeth against the big wooden banister at the bottom of the stairs. I laid in a minuscule, yet effective, pool of my own blood for what seemed like an hour, but that's how much I loved them. I would have killed myself for those toys, and despite the fact that half my face looked like an eggplant, I gathered up enough strength to lift my head up off the floor when they finally came through the front door to gasp, "What did you bring me?"

And that's exactly what kind of aunt I set out to be. I wanted that kid to figuratively throw himself down a flight of stairs because he loves me so bad. But this child, blood of my blood, flesh of my flesh, considered my love a vile, *vile* thing.

"Nicholas," my sister beckoned from the front seat, "Give Aunt Laurie a kiss. Please. PLEASE."

His expression drew upwards and then back, he uttered a high-pitched "OH, WHY?" and them promptly burst into tears, thrashing his head back and forth and finally pummeling the armrest of his car seat with a pudgy fist.

I briefly entertained the thought of saying, "I paid for that kiss with that $19.95 Tarzan Tree House Playset I just bought you!" but instead, I got my self together, choked back the tears and simply waved good-bye.

I called him when I got home, just to make sure that things were still okay between us, but my sister relayed that he couldn't come to the phone, although I heard him happily playing in the background.

"He says he has a headache," she told me.

Several days later, we met at my Nana's to have supper, and Nicholas greeted me at the door, wearing a felt loincloth of sorts, a necklace of plastic teeth and carrying a spear.

"AAAAAAAHHHH!" he yelled, beating on his bare little chest. "I'm TARZAN! You be tiger!"

Thinking that we had made tremendous strides since it had been publicly announced that my mouth held the appeal of an ashtray, I quickly agreed, hunkering down on all fours.

"Bad tiger!" he yelled as all 34 pounds of him leapt from the couch onto my back with the herniated disk.

"I'M GONNA TO GET YOU, TIGER!" he shrieked, running from the far corner of the room and body slamming me.

"Bad tiger to get out Nana's house!" he said, picking up two wooden drumsticks from his play wagon and pointing them at my eyes.

"Wait!" I screamed as he came running toward me. "Could we not use props, please?"

"What's props?" he asked me.

"Anything that can make Aunt Laurie bleed or result in her wearing diapers and living at Grandma's house again," I answered.

"Nicholas," my sister called. "It's time for supper, get dressed now."

"Come on, Lord of the Flies," I said as looked for his real clothes. "Let's get you changed."

"NOOO!!!" he screamed with all of his might. "Not Aunt Laurie!"

"Why?" my sister asked.

Truth is, I never saw it coming.

"She too FAT," he said, then turned and pointed to my belly.

The room suddenly stood still. No one—my sister, my brother-in-law, my nana, me—no one said a word.

"Nicholas," my sister finally said quietly between clenched teeth, "Say you're sorry."

He didn't mean it, he's THREE, I told myself as I realized that maybe I really was one meal away from being trapped inside my house, spending the remainder of my days on a king size bed with dirty sheets, hugging a bucket of chicken.

Nicholas lifted his little shoulders in a shrug and said, "I'm sorry you fat, Aunt Laurie."

"Don't worry about trying to find a big enough casket when my fat finally kills me," I said to my family. "Just drain mom and dad's pool, roll me in and fill it in with some gravel. I'm totally fine with that."

"He's three," my sister said with a weak grin.

"I know," I said, shaking my head. "But how much more can I take?"

"Six to nine pounds more?" she added, pointing to her belly. "By next March?"

I thought about it, nodding. Eight months? I smiled. I could probably

12

lose some weight by then.

Allergic

It's 12:36 a.m., my eyes fly wide open and I find myself gasping for breath. I look at the clock and realize that it's only been three minutes since the last time I've blown my nose. I find my tissue and blow until I hear my ears pop.

I'm not sick.

I have allergies.

It's 1:07 a.m., my eyes fly open, I gasp for breath, it's been a minute and a half since I've blown my nose. I feel for my tissue and blow until I think I've dislodged an eye.

I have bad allergies.

It's 2:14 a.m., I'm awake, I can't breathe and I can't find my tissue. I blow my nose on my T-shirt until I wake the dogs and my husband rolls over and blindly bats his hands at me.

I am dying.

It's 2:15 a.m., I wander down the dark hallway, step in a pile of fresh puppy doody and proceed to the bathroom, where I look into the mirror and try to determine if either of my nostrils is large enough to accept the nozzle of the vacuum cleaner.

I haven't slept in excess of an hour in almost three weeks, since the morning when I woke up and thought that someone had poured the foundation of a house into my nose. Every time I breathe in, my sinuses sound like I'm about to complete a magic trick. If I breathe out, my nose whistles and my mouth wheezes. I'm one big histamine accordion.

"You are the unhealthiest person I know," my mother said over the phone. "That's what you get for eating nothing but sugar!"

"I'm not sick," I protested. "I have allergies!"

"Why are you listening to polka music?" she asked.

"I'm not," I answered weakly. "That's my respiratory system."

"I thought I heard a drum roll," she mentioned.

"That would be my left nostril," I added. "My right one sounds more like a tambourine."

I'm well into my thirties, have lived in Arizona since 1972 and have never had this kind of reaction to my environment before. Ever. I've had allergies for a day here and there, but nothing like this. As a result, there is enough pressure in my head to cook a pot roast, and I've taken to wearing two rolls of Charmin around my wrists like bracelets. When I sneezed the day before last, something came out of my head that was so big that I got scared and tried to put it back.

"You get sick more than anyone I know," my friend Louise said. "It's because you eat chocolate like it was a vitamin!"

"I'm not sick," I argued. "I have allergies! And if something makes you happy, you should eat it!"

"Louise told me all about your eating habits," my friend Jim said. "No wonder you're so sick all of the time. Please wear this mask if you want to respond to me."

"It's not like I eat rat poop," I said, slipping the mask over my mouth. "I don't have the Plague. It's allergies! And for your information, a Milky Way a day is *not that much*!"

Several days ago, my neighbor told me a joke and as I started to laugh, I felt my nose give birth to a snot bubble that grew to the size of a tennis ball before it erupted and left a big shiny mark on my cheek. I have taken more medication than Doris Duke, ingesting the equivalent to an eight ball of TheraFlu, Afrin and Extra-Strength Sudafed each day. I wondered why I was crying during Party of Five until I understood that the tears were coming from my nose, and it was at that point that I abandoned the rolls of Charmin and started carrying a towel.

Things were getting bad, and I didn't even know what I was allergic *to*. It was just something *out there*. At least with a cold, I could see a light at the end of the tunnel. But with this, there was no salvation, and I couldn't even identify the enemy. It was just going to go on forever. From now on, I would have to live my life with two wads of toilet paper planted in each nasal opening; the shiny red sheen my upper lip that had begin to develop from the excessive use of paper towels; and in a constant antihistamine stupor which often left me staring at the plaster patterns on my walls, imagining that I saw freaky little devil faces. The only other thing

I could do was lay on the couch and watch TV, flipping myself over every half an hour to let each nostril drain.

"Hey, Linus Sinus," my husband said tonight as we were getting ready for bed. "Get your Booger Blanket off my side. It's coming dangerously close to my pillow."

"I hate you," I replied, pulling the Booger Blanket closer to me.

"Big words from a little lady with feminine hygiene products shoved up her nose," he said as he laughed at me.

"They're not tampons!" I shouted. "They're tissue plugs so I don't drown in my own fluids!"

"Well, those things better not fall out at night!" he asserted. "I don't want to get sick."

"I'm not sick!" I yelled. "I have allergies! Just look at me! My eyes are so swollen I can't find my eyelids! I'm pretty sure that I saw a chunk of my short-term memory in a wad of toilet paper! I've become a MOUTH BREATHER. This is not sick! With sick you can get better. Allergies are FOREVER."

"You are so cranky," my husband said.

"I'm cranky?" I gulped. "Well let me stick two gummy bears up your nose and see how jolly you are!"

"If I roll over and see that you're letting your nose drip all over my pillow, you're in big trouble," my husband said as he pointed to me. "And I don't want to wake up and find one of those snot pellets next to my mouth or anything. Because I will freak. Out."

At 2:27 a.m., I wake from a dream that the nose tampons have stretched my nostrils wide enough to accept the corner attachment of the vacuum cleaner if I clip off most of the bristles.

The next morning, when my husband calls out from the other end of the house to ask me why the vacuum cleaner is in the bathroom, I get out of bed to investigate.

"I have no idea," I say as I stand in the doorway.

"Oh no," he says, holding a nose tampon in one hand and pointing to a wadded up tissue in the waste basket with the other. "I think that's the part of your brain that stores phone numbers! What have you done?"

"Who knows?" I reply, throwing up my hands. "But listen to this pair of clear nostrils!"

I just ordered $48 worth of Prilosec and 36 rolls of Charmin Blue to be delivered to me on a Sunday because.... I just could. I can't decide if I'm awesome or an asshole.

Foolin' Around

If you told me last week that I'd take my clothes off for millions of people to see and get paid for it, I'd tell you, "Get outta here! Quit your fooling around!"

Hey, who knew? The last person I expected to hear on the other end of the phone line was Kevin, the photo editor I had interviewed while covering the auditions for the Playmate 2000 contest last year. Against my better judgment during our interview, he talked me into auditioning for the contest myself, and I did it, despite the fact that the other girls in the room looked like they were all hatched from one egg laid by Pamela Anderson. There was enough silicone in that room to seal every bathtub drain in the continental United States. And yea, as I walked through the Valley of the Shadow of Breasts wearing a white bathrobe with an embroidered bunny on the lapel, my inner thighs rubbing together and creating one really painful rash, for the rest of my life, I could truthfully say that I had tried out to be a Playboy centerfold.

I never expected them to call. During the audition, I never even took my clothes off. When it was my turn and I disrobed, the photographer saw me in my gray jumper and black tights, he shot me a puzzled look.

"I wasn't expecting to...try out," I explained, laying across the bed like a corpse. "I'm not really...ready."

"Don't worry," the photographer coaxed. "I've seen everything!"

"No, no," I said, shaking my head. "No, you haven't. You see I haven't shaved—"

"I've seen stubble," he interrupted, laughing.

"—since the morning of my wedding in 1996," I finished. "Naked, I'm a tourist attraction from Rwanda."

Apparently, however, the fact that I remained clothed didn't kill my chances, in fact, it increased them. Over the phone last week, Kevin explained that my modesty was "very alluring" and "intriguing," something the folks at Playboy don't see very often.

"We see girls every day, giving looksies away for free," he added. "There's no challenge in that! But you, you're like a private reserve. Carefully keeping nature's bounty a secret, you know?"

"Nature has been very bountiful to me," I added, nodding my head and feeling my second and third chins dance together. "Will you pay for liposuction?"

"Are you kidding?" Kevin yelled into the receiver. "We love you just the way you are. You are EVERY WOMAN. We narrowed down our search to you and Monica Lewinsky, but you are more 'EVERY.' Do you know how sick I am of Skinny Minnies? If I see another protruding ribcage, I'm going to throw it on the grill and slap some KC Masterpiece on it!"

"Really?" I said, giggling. "Because I was about to eat a Twinkie!"

"Eat the Twinkie!" Kevin shouted joyfully. "Eat a Ding Dong! The tide is changing, girlfriend, and you are going to be the poster girl for the Real Woman of the New Millennium!"

"I have a zit on my neck the size of a cat's eye marble," I added.

"If it has a shadow, we can airbrush," he replied. "But we'd rather keep our Nude Real Woman of the New Millennium as very real as possible."

I stopped. I had forgotten about the naked part.

"Kevin," I mentioned carefully, "Do I have to be totally naked? I mean, can I have some props, like a rug, or a big poncho?"

"Well, you have that thing on your neck, but of course we can work in other props," he said, much to my relief. "How about a book? Or a feather? And don't freak out, you won't be totally naked. You'll be wearing pearls!"

That was still pretty NAKED. Could I do NAKED? Even for money? I really didn't know.

I thought back to all the letters I received a couple of weeks ago, calling me "sick," "repressed," "Victorian" and a "disgusting pig" because I freaked out when I saw a naked lady in the locker room. Maybe the angry naked people were right, I said to myself suddenly. Maybe my body was God's art, maybe everything I was taught about modesty, privacy and propriety was wrong. Maybe I should start letting it all hang out, even the wrinkled parts. Maybe I should show my respect for my body by being intimate with strangers. Maybe pride really is taking off my clothes for people I don't know and will never meet! In the name of God's beautiful creation, I could make my privates into an open house! Especially for the right dollar amount!

So I went to work creating the all-important bio of myself that would run with my pictorial, exposing more of my inner self to Playboy's readers than what would already be in the layout, especially the one of me climbing rocks:

Favorite color: Fudge

Hobby: Chicken Fried Steak

Lifetime Goal: To outlaw any dress size under 12 and get the original cream filling back into Twinkies, Ding Dongs and Sno Balls

Turn offs: Climbing rocks with no panties on

Turn ons: Popping the zit on my neck on the first try

I also practiced cursive writing, dotting each "I" with a smiley face and crossing each "T" with a full, pouty set of lips. After I finished my bio, I had to do the hardest thing of all, and that was tell my mom. I didn't want her hearing about my lay out at her Bunko club after she had just eaten a forkful of Ambrosia salad. I had to call her myself.

"Mom, I'm going to be Playboy's Nude Real Woman of the New Millennium!" I tired to say as excitedly, quietly and quickly as possible.

"That's too bad," she said rather calmly. "Because I don't think the pictures will turn out too good because of the casts."

"The casts for what?" I asked.

"The casts the doctor puts on both of your legs after I break them like pretzels!" she yelled. "How sexy is that, Miss Open To The Public? Huh? I'm sending you back to that doctor for some more counseling, because if you think you're going to ruin this family's name, you're NUTS, you hear me? Your brain's the size of a damn walnut if you think you're showing your patootey and lentils to strange men!"

"Take it easy. It's very tasteful, Mom. I'm wearing pearls!" I said adamantly. "Besides, April is the cruelest month. Especially the first day."

Arizona Survival Kit

When you move to California, it's common knowledge that you should buy or prepare an earthquake kit. If you live in Tornado Alley, chances are you have the supplies and required items on hand to get you through the storm season in your Scaredy Hole.

But when you move to Phoenix, the only primer you'll get is, "It's a dry heat." The old-timers (anyone who has survived one summer in the desert) will sit by and watch the newcomers try to deal with complexities of July in Arizona as they innocently touch the handle of a shopping cart that's been sitting in the sun for three hours in a parking lot of melting asphalt. True, it's some great, cheap entertainment, but after you've seen approximately 1400 people burn their hands on an 800-degree metal rod, it tends to lose some of its magic.

Let's face it, we only have two seasons "hot" and "hotter," and in some native tongues, the word "Phoenix" translates into "What is known as Hell, but with an occasional garden hose." If you don't know the proper protocol of desert life, our town will kill you in about sixteen minutes flat, but you can easily cut that time in half if you're wearing black.

Consider the following a guide to an Arizona Summer Survival Kit, and use it wisely. If you don't, we all reserve the right to laugh at you in the parking lot at Fry's. Because we will.

1: You will need WATER. Especially if you plan to travel more than three feet from your front door. I figure if you step foot on a mountain without several barrels of Arrowhead strapped to your waist, you deserve nothing less than to pop up on the news as you're strapped to a basket attached to a helicopter. In Phoenix, we have a name for people who do that. They're called IDIOTS. They don't call it a "dry heat" for nothing!

2: You will need an oven mitt, and I would suggest investing in a high quality one. You will use it in order to push a grocery cart, to open your car door and to touch your steering wheel. In a pinch, maxi pads with a sticky strip will do, but if you plan on dish toweling it, you're just playing with fire. One summer, I cooked a brisket in my glove box and a bag of potting soil was fired into a stepping stone when my car spontaneously acted as a kiln. If a dishtowel is the only protection between your hand and a steering wheel hot enough to cremate it, I hope you work well with hooks.

    3: You will need several bags of frozen peas and carrots for each member of your family, because when the monsoon knocks your electricity out for three days, only the cool will survive. Peas and carrots work especially well since they can be molded and will slip nicely into the cups of bras and other tender spots.

    4: You will need a job that provides air conditioning. If the place where you sit for eight hours a day isn't air conditioned, quit. If they provide evaporative cooling, laugh at them and *then* quit. Even some motorcycle cops have been known to take sabbaticals for the summer only to turn up working the shake machine at Jack-in-the-Box. If it ain't cool inside, it just ain't cool.

    5: You will need real deodorant and antiperspirant. This is not a buffet, you cannot pick one and forgo the other. YOU NEED BOTH. And that herbal crap from the health food store or the hippie rock people rub in their armpits DOES NOT CUT IT. You may feel PC, but you smell like something that stepped out of a Diana Gabaldon novel. Science has advanced for a reason, people. Get something with chemicals in it! The more frightening the warning label on it, the better it will work.

    6: You will need a leash. Well, maybe that's too harsh--let's call it a "Desert Lifeline" for an elder member of your family who has looked at you funny at least once. I can't explain whey the scrubland has such an appeal for those who are slightly challenged in the memory department, but it does, and before you know it, someone on the picnic is missing and most likely scrambling toward a cactus. Stay safe. Stay tethered.

    7: You will need to understand that the name stamped on the motor of your car is not Evinrude. When the monsoon hits, people get *swept away*, driving their vehicles straight into washes and riverbeds as if lured there by a swami. They enter swollen, flooded streets in Monte Carlos and El Caminos, steering them like they were pontoon boats. When the floorboards start to leak, they scramble to the roofs until a helicopter with some rope shows up. In Phoenix, we have a name for people who do that. They're called DRIPPING IDIOTS.

8: You will need to ignore most of the weather people. They will crack open eggs and fry them on sidewalks, try to cook a whole Denny's Grand Slam on a driveway and then poke at it like monkeys around a termite hill. Sometimes, they clap. Refrain from this activity. The sidewalk is NOT nature's griddle. No one in Phoenix cooks this way unless they went to weather man school, and should you happen to fry an egg on the sidewalk, recent legislation requires that you must now also eat it.

Please feel free to pass this information to other new people you come across—well, except for the oven mitt part. After all, don't you deserve a little laughter, too?

I just got upset about a not good review on Amazon for my book, but then when I saw that the person also gave three stars to grass seed and a rag rug, I felt much better.

Oy Veda

Honestly, I don't know what I was thinking and crossed the threshold of an upscale make-up store and stood there under the white, revealing fluorescent lights.

I don't know what possessed me. But there I was, already in the store before my folly hit me square in the jaw as every sales rep (i.e.: clerk) stopped what they were doing to turn around and stare at me.

I knew instantly that I had made a huge mistake.

I felt like I had entered a room brimming with flawless, Amazon queens who were now watching the ape girl clamber about their store, her hairy knuckles grazing on the bleached wood floors. They looked at me like I had just escaped from my cage at the zoo and was heading straight for the snack bar in search of raw hot dogs. Only one of them, a skinny little red-headed freckled girl, understood enough to give me a sympathetic smile.

Caught like a raccoon chomping on a pre-eaten corn cob in a trash can, I knew it was too late to run. Instead, I just played along, strolling leisurely in front of the shelves, pretending to look at stuff. The sales reps simply kept their distance, eyeing my every move, convinced, I'm sure, that the only plausible reason for my being in their store was to rob them or ask them to call 911 and then promptly have a seizure.

What was I thinking, I asked myself, now under surveillance, what was I thinking? Did I think that simply because I had finally gotten my eyebrows waxed that I could now join the ranks of the perfect girls? Did I think that just because I had resisted picking at the zit that resembled a Hot Tamale between my eyes for an *entire day* that I could walk among the exquisite, unnoticed? It was obvious that I didn't deserve to be in their store. I had not earned it.

It wasn't until I picked up a sample tube of mascara and began to fiddle with it did one of the perfect girls approach me. Admittedly, I was struggling with the tube being that my kind hasn't evolved yet to the point of bearing opposable thumbs. Not a second too soon, the sales girl pulled the mascara out of my hand before I moved onto Plan B, which was to wrench the container open with my nasty, yellow, chimp teeth. She was the biggest of the perfect girls, and I had a feeling she was sent out to distract me while the size two and size four sales girls went to secure a dart gun to bring me down with.

"Can I help you?" she said, looking at me like I was shedding, and replaced the mascara in it's proper spot.

Although I was tempted to suddenly begin flashing my hands around in an attempt to communicate in monkey language that "Koko want to choke you with big primate hand," Koko decided to take the higher road.

"I'm thinking about buying A LOT of make-up," I said with a smile. "Do you work on commission?"

"Yes, we do," the sales rep said, suddenly melting into an expression that even this gorilla girl could understand, "fake nice."

"Good," I said with a nod. "Then I want the red-headed girl to help me."

The freckled nice girl smiled again and came forth, armed with a triangular sponge.

"I'm going to blend the foundation," she added as she went to work and dabbed some make-up onto my nose. "Wow, how many times did you have this pierced?"

I stuttered, about to say "never," until I realized that she was talking about my pores, which are apparently so large that they can be seen on satellite photographs. So I laughed quickly and said, "Oh, you know, the real lesson there is not to let your friends near your head with a needle after they've gotten friendly with a bottle of Cuervo Gold!"

Then the red-haired girl swooped in closer to work on my eyebrows, and luckily, I had just taken a big breath. I was going to have to hold it, the girl was too close for me to exhale my exhaust-pipe breath on her. Then immediately, I was struck with a horrible thought: I think I smell like an onion. A big, yellow, stinky onion, even though I hadn't eaten any. Please God, I pleaded, please don't let me smell. Sometimes an onion stench can trail you for weeks, it can creep up on you like a whitehead! Oh God! I added, please don't let me have any whiteheads!

If the red-headed girl caught a whiff of my stench, she was nice enough not to say anything as she finished my eyebrows and stepped back just when I was about to pass out from oxygen deprivation.

"Are you okay?" the red-haired girl said as I started to cough and catch my breath. I nodded, still coughing.

"Are you having a seizure?" she asked, to which I shook my head.

"Okay, take a look," she added, holding up a mirror in which not Liza Minnelli, but a Liza Minnelli male impersonator looked back at me. I had eyebrows that reached clear to my ears and a mouth that looked like I had been hit in the face with a red paintball. I would have gasped had I not been so busy trying to stay alive.

"Can you believe the improvement?" she said. "Now that will be $150.25."

I choked one more time. "Seizure! Seizure!" I rattled.

Babies

When my friend Amy leaned over the table and announced during our lunch that she was going to have a baby, I didn't even blink.

"Great," I said nodding my head. "It was nice knowing you!"

You see, my friends are quickly dropping off one by one. In the last two years, I've lost more friends to babies than I did to booze. It's amazing and horrifying at the same time, since my friend number has dwindled so dramatically that statistically speaking, it should be war time.

Okay, so I guess having babies is simply nature at work. I understand that. There's a sense of immortality connected with it. But so is waking up with a hangover and a cold hot dog down your pants, I want to argue, what about that? That's something you never live down, that story will be kept alive for generations of bar flies to come. Real legends never die! They just go to detox!

Suffice it to say that when my first friend fell into the parenthood pit, I wasn't prepared at all. When Mark, one of my best friends since college, told me that his wife, Marcie, was pregnant, I was thrilled that I finally had a reason to buy the tiny clothes I coveted in the window of Baby Gap. Mark had a daughter named Bethany. And that was that.

Apparently, the parenthood handbook states in bold print the moment anyone gains a baby, they lose the skill required to dial anyone else's phone number aside from their mother's. I found this out the hard way, all the while thinking that I had done something wrong, that maybe Mark thought I bought the baby clothes on the clearance rack, or worse, he had found out what I had said about him to another of our friends.

Anyway, I finally got a hold of him at work, and I was really excited because I had some gold caliber gossip to pass on.

"....and when he said, 'You gave me crabs!' she said she got them from sitting in a taxi cab!" I laughed maniacally into the phone receiver. "Can you believe that? Taxi cab crabs! Ha ha ha!"

"Oh! Guess what?" Mark suddenly interjected. "When I went to get her up this morning, Bethany was standing there, just waiting for me. She looked at me like, 'Hey! Where have you been?' I just died laughing!"

"Yeah," I mentioned simply. "Sounds just like an episode of Seinfeld."

"Oh, you should see her!" Mark continued. "The doctor says we have to wean her soon, but she's the best suckler he's ever seen. She just latches onto Marcie like a vacuum cleaner. She's in the 99th percentile!"

I was aghast. I hadn't heard such talk since the last time I drank margaritas and dialed a 1-900 number. Suckling, weaning, latching! Who wanted to know that kind of stuff? I certainly didn't. Nor did I want the visual accompaniment of a topless Marcie holding a baby with a mouth that had the properties of a black hole.

My friend was gone; he had simply moved on. I felt like I was Beta and everyone left me for VHS. There was a new game in town, I realized, and unless I was prepared to take on a renter in my uterus, I wasn't even allowed to play. I couldn't compete with a baby, especially an advanced one that ranked at the top of its class! How could I win against that? In high school I had to repeat Essential Math Skills twice and I still feel nauseous when I see fractions.

Then, when Mark said he couldn't come to my book signing because Bethany's one-year old best friend was having a birthday party at the Railroad Park with a "big bouncy house and everything," I finally got it. It was the same kind of feeling I had when I finally realized my youngest sister was a mother when she popped up one day wearing a green macaroni necklace and a bracelet of dried peas. Up until that point, she had just been my sister who had been baby-sitting for a very long time. Mark was now a dad. And I had been knocked out of the friendship loop by his baby, even though I had known him way longer and had seen him dead drunk with a hot dog down his pants (it seemed very funny when I put it there).

In time, more and more of my friends stood on the edge of the parenting cliff and jumped off. "Good-bye, it was nice knowing you!" I'd wave, dumping out a beer and smoking a cigarette in memory of my homies who had passed on to the other side. Soon, I looked around and only a few soldiers were left standing. I invested most of my energy in Cindy and Maura, two of my friends that I had hooked up due to my talent as a yenta for lesbians (I figured if they ever got married, I had doubled my chances for being "Goddess of Honor"). I knew they wouldn't disappoint me; they'd stick with their barren friend until the bitter end.

That is, until I hadn't heard from them in a while and finally gave them a call.

"We got a puppy!" Maura cried with glee. "And when I woke up this morning, he was standing in the kitchen, giving me this look that said, 'Hey! Where have you been?' I just died laughing!"

"Don't forget to tell her," I heard Cindy yell in the background. "that he's in the 99th percentile!"

It's confirmed. I really am an idiot. Somehow, my cursor jumped size from a regular arrow to a BIG arrow, and I shrieked, believing it to be an enormous black fly that was skating around my computer screen in circles. In the same circles I was moving my finger.

BATTER BATTER BATTER

It was a blustery night.

Dark clouds had rolled over us in a matter of minutes, and the wind had picked up enough that I was glad I wasn't wearing a skirt. As we walked through the narrow streets of downtown toward the Bank One Ballpark, the wind blew papers, leaves and dust all around us.

I was kind of excited. It was going to be my first baseball game, and I really wanted to see the stadium that all of those old people lost their houses for.

My sister had some free tickets passed to her and was going with some friends, so I decided, why not. I'll go.

"If you're going to a baseball game, there's something I have to tell you," my husband said when I told him.

"We're not going to Chicago so you can tell me that you've been having an affair with six of my best friends on the Jerry Springer Show and that I have to hit all of them, are you?" I said hesitantly.

"No," he answered.

"Or that you're a man living as a woman living as a man," I said wincing. "You can't borrow my shoes. Your feet are way too wide."

"No," he said again.

"Did we win the doublewide trailer in the Jerry Springer contest?" I said, my eyes getting big.

"You really have to get a job," he replied. "No. This has nothing to do with Jerry Springer. It has to do with your head. And flying baseballs. You need to keep alert, because if a baseball is going to hit anybody, it's going to hit you. And we don't have insurance."

"You mean I have a big head," I whimpered. "A big pumpkin head. A head so big that things can't help but smash into it. A big head on a little pin body."

"Just keep your eyes open," he warned.

I was remembering this as we neared the stadium, the wind blowing strong, and was relaying this to my sister. I had just finished saying, "If you had to guess, how many pies do you think my head would yield," when I saw him. It. Them.

Big wide eyes, irises as big as quarters. Huge, piney teeth. Clacking jaw. A revolving head.

I sucked in all of my breath without even knowing it and my sister grabbed my arm. She knows.

"Don't look," she warned, because as afraid as I am of clowns, there's an even greater terror out there, and it was zeroing in on me. "Don't look," she repeated in a whisper, and led me away from the person on the corner and the talking dummy that was cradled in the crook of their arm.

"Hey Lady!" the dummy yelled. "Lady with the white shirt and the buttons! Hey Lady, come over here!"

I felt sick. He, the dummy, IT, was talking to me. Yelling at me. Trying to get me to come close to it.

"Hey Lady! I've got something to tell you! Come over here!"

"WHY?" I yelled back as I turned my head. "So you can suck the eyeballs out of my humongous head with your little wooden mouth?"

"If you don't say anything else to the doll," my sister shot, "I'll buy you cotton candy."

"And a four-dollar hot dog?" I asked, walking faster.

Inside, she made good on her offer, and also bought me peanuts and a pretzel, but for that I had to promise not to swear in front of her friends. I bought my own $4 soda.

We found our tiny little plastic seats, which placed me precariously close to a stranger who was eating a mustard-slathered polish sausage with only what looked like three teeth. Bank One signs lit up all over the place, and that's when I realized that with charges generated from my bounced checks, I bet I financed every row of section 119's Tupperware chairs.

First I ate the $4 hot dog, which really didn't taste any different than the package of Corn Boy hot dogs we buy at Fry's for .99 on a good week. Then I ate the $3.50 pretzel, and there wasn't anything special about that either, except that it made me drink the rest of my soda. My sister made me share the $4.50 bag of peanuts. Then I dug into the $4.50 cotton candy which looked and tasted a lot like the insulation I just had installed in my attic.

Suddenly, my eyes slammed shut and my hand flew to my nose to pinch it closed, but it was too late. The sneeze erupted, unleashed and unbound, followed by ten more. My sinuses were swelling quickly, filling the cavernous space of my gigantic skull as a result of a vicious allergy attack from the afternoon's wind. The three-toothed woman looked at me accusingly as she gummed the remnants of the bun, so I just sat there for a long time, my eyes closed and my nose wrapped in a napkin, trying not to sneeze.

I sat that way until the moment when my intestines seized. Like a python contracting in my lower torso, they pulsed and squeezed, tying themselves into painful knots. I knew I was in trouble. Big trouble. Cotton candy, four-dollar hot dog, peanut and pretzel eaten in the span of fifteen-minute sort of trouble. I was far away from my private throne at home, stuck in a very public place with very public restrooms and a seeping nose and cramps.

"We gotta go!" I whispered hastily into my sister's ear.

"Are you crazy?" she said. "The game hasn't started yet! I'm not leaving now!"

"I'm going to be sick," I almost yelled.

"Then go to the bathroom," she said, brushing me off.

"It's too public," I complained. "Give me the keys to your car. I'll drove home and back before the game is over."

"No way," she said. "You're not a very good driver and Dad just bought me that car."

"Dad bought you that car?" I said, shocked. "I thought I was next up! I haven't had a new car since—"

"You totaled your last car," she said. "That's why you got his old one."

"That's not my car!" I protested. "It's just a loaner until he buys me a new one!"

"Yeah, no," she informed me. "That's not a loaner. That is your car. You've had it for three years. You're going to have to go to rehab before he buys you a new one."

"That is *not* my car," I pouted. "There are cigarette burns on the roof. I would never have done that if I knew it was my car. Just give me your keys!"

"Now that I know you burn holes in the ceilings of cars you don't think are yours, no," she said and then just ignored me.

"You're going to make me use the bathroom here?" I asked, incredulously.

"You just ate forty-five dollars' worth of concession snacks in fifteen minutes," she replied. "What did you think was going to happen? There's not even a competitive eating category for that, it's so dangerous!"

My window of opportunity for a respectable getaway was closing quickly, too quickly. As my lower GI system turned itself into a sailor's knot, I jumped up, an avalanche of food crumbs tumbling to the floor like a snack blizzard.

"If I'm not back by half-time, call my husband and get the member ID number from the insurance card and then call 911," I told her before I ran up the stairs and shouted randomly at people "Restroom! Restroom!" until one finally pointed to an opening in the wall that women were streaming in and out of.

I ran to it like a homing pigeon. I bumped into people, caused one guy to lose some of his popcorn to the ground, and I was so desperate I didn't even think to stop and try to catch and eat the morsels that tumbled from his bucket.

All I knew was that in each passing moment, I grew closer and closer to a moment that could never be undone, and I was so focused on finding a bathroom stall that I probably didn't hear it at first.

The sound of wood hitting wood, as if a child had wandered into the lavatory with two blocks, banging them together,

Then the sound came closer, and closer, until it was in the stall next to me, the clacking getting louder.

"Hey Lady," a raspy, wooden voice hissed. "I bet you could eat five pies out of that enormous skull of yours."

I flushed to smother the sound of my cries, and then hunkered down and waited for the ambulance to come.

OUT OF THE AREA

If you're from the wrong side of the tracks and you're thinking about getting fancy and writing a check at a Basha's, our local grocery store chain, on the right side of the tracks, you'd better think again.

You're not only out of your mind, you're OUT OF THE AREA as well.

The Sunday before last I was picking up some things my Nana asked me to get as I was on my way to her house for dinner. So I stopped into Basha's and picked up some bread, brownies and a package of hot dogs I thought I'd make for supper the following night.

But as all of my stuff was swiped through the scanner, I realized that my debit card was not in my wallet. It's cool, I thought to myself, it's probably just floating around in my purse somewhere, I'll just write a check. No big deal.

Right.

When the cashier, who had a growth on her face the size and shape of a cashew, looked at my check, she got a puzzled expression on her face. "Where's this?" she said, and then spouted off my address.

"Oh," I said, not even thinking about it. "That's downtown."

Now, by the next series of events that happened, you would have thought that I signed that check "Laurie bin Laden," because all of a sudden, the intercom was flipped on, the light above the cashier began to pulse and *the manager was called.*

Still, I wasn't worried. My mom shopped at that Basha's since I was a kid and when I lived in the area before we moved downtown, I shopped at that Basha's, too, and have written checks there for a good 15 years without incident (if a check eventually clears without intervention from the state attorney general, I consider that "without incident").

Until now.

When the manager examined the check and then disappeared into his secret Bat Cave with it, I started to feel that something wasn't right. After five solid minutes of waiting while the line at the check-out grew steadily behind me, I finally looked at the cashier who was busy clearing all of the crud out from underneath her fingernails with the end of a stubby little pencil. Now pay attention to the following repartee, because it's one of the most stunning examples of complete and exquisite inefficiency and bad management that I have ever encountered, in the wild or otherwise.

"What seems to be the problem?" I asked the cashier.

"You're out of the area," she replied without looking at me.

"Excuse me?" I responded. "What does that mean?"

"It means that you're out of the area," she repeated. "You live too far away. It's a new policy."

"For what? I live in *Phoenix*!" I said, shaking my head. "We have Basha's downtown, too, you know."

"I don't know that for a fact," she snipped.

"Well I do, it's the filthiest store in the neighborhood," I added. "And I've been writing checks at this Basha's for at least 15 years,"

"Well I don't recognize you," she said snottily.

Unfortunately, I wanted so badly to add, I don't have a distinguishing and memorable feature, such as a dry-roasted legume, sprouting out of my head.

Then I didn't have a light bulb moment, as Oprah calls it. I had a floodlight moment.

"Oh, I get it," I said, nodding. "I get it now. I have a *ghetto* address. I have a poor person's address. Look at that! That zip code has TWO ZEROES in it! Why the nerve of me to come to this store so obviously OUT OF MY AREA and try to write a check!"

After 15 minutes of waiting for the manager to return, I reached into my pocket to grab my pen and start taking notes, and that's when I felt my lost debit card.

"Call your manager and get my check back," I said as I swiped the debit card through the terminal. "But don't bother file my face in your brain's check approval section, because I I'm sure your cameras have already caught it and are making fliers with my picture on them right now to alert everyone that I live downtown, and not across the street at the mobile home park where a guy was found in his recliner after he had been dead for three years."

She handed me my approved receipt, I grabbed the bags full of Nana's stuff and turned around just in time to see the manager coming towards me.

"There are insufficient funds in this account," he informed me and everyone else at the check-out.

"What?" I said as I laughed, knowing full well that my debit card and my checks are drawn from the exact same account. "That is not true!"

"That's what the bank said," he insisted. "And I talked to a real live person!"

"How do you know you can trust her?" I replied. "Did you get her zip code? She might just be an operative working from OUT OF THE AREA, you know!"

"Well, here's your bad check," the manager said, handing it to me.

"It's too bad you think that," I declared. "Because this was the good one. But thanks for the tip, because when I need to stock up on filet mignons, lobster, wine and lottery tickets, I'll make sure to use a check with a Scottsdale address. And write it out to Safeway."

I was just at Safeway, and the guy in front of me only had one, crooked, gnarly tiny carrot. In a bag. That's all he had. And I kept looking at it. And laughing. And looking at it. And laughing, and finally, I was simply forced to ask, "What are you going to do with one awful, tiny carrot?" He raised his eyebrows and said, "Getting cash." "Oh," I said. "Thank God."

Big Bad Bella

In some tragedies, you can rebuild, you can start over, you can move to a new town. But when you let evil into your house, give it a bed and something to eat, you're just kind of stuck with it for as long as it wants to stay.

When we hear bumps in the night, my husband and I know it is The Evil. When we see objects fly across the room in broad daylight and when our bed shakes violently every morning as the sun breaks through the sky, we know it is The Evil.

We know it is, because we can roll over and see The Evil dripping gobs of foamy saliva onto our sheets as its eyes, black as coal and shiny as diamonds, bore right into us.

My husband and I willingly brought The Evil into our home, but at the time, it was wearing a disguise. Dressed in a little brown fur coat, sad, droopy eyes and boasting a tiny pink tongue, The Evil shape-shifted itself into a puppy and passed over our threshold as my birthday present last year.

We named her Bella, which in Italian, means "beautiful," but in dog is a direct translation of "Nosferatu."

As we slept that night, Bella took the time to fully develop into a weapon of mass destruction, and when we woke the next morning we shuffled through the remains of what used to be our home.

A roll of toilet paper met its death after encountering Bella's set of little knives the Devil implanted in her mouth as teeth, shreds of white still fluttered in the air. My husband's left shoe groaned in the corner after being mutilated beyond recognition. Her wicker bed, fresh and new only the day before, was reduced to a pile of skeletal shards. A bottle of Tums tried to limp to safety, it's cap severed from its crushed and now splintered body, with half of its innards eaten.

I placed a call to my vet that morning, telling a technician that my three-pound dog had consumed her weight in brightly colored antacids.

"Keep an eye on her," the tech told me. "If she starts acting strange, bring her in."

"If she *starts* acting strange?" I thought to myself as the puppy gnawed my pinkie toe down to the bone. What does she need to do to fill that requirement? She's already tasted blood. One gruesome day, my husband will come home to find me half-eaten, because this is the dog that won't wait until I take my last breath to sink her Henckels into the filet mignons that are my thighs.

Keeping Bella under surveillance, however, did not become an option, and I did it every time Bella feasted on a package of Sudafed, including the foil blister packs; approximately seven cigarettes, including the filters; 12 sticks of Trident, a book of matches and a tube of Monistat 7.

As time passed, Bella morphed from a puppy into a creature that should have had top-billing in *The Howling*. We tried to keep the destruction to a minimum by providing the little monster with toys and an endless supply of rawhide chews, bones that Bella entertains herself with by throwing them up in the air like ninja stars, knocking pictures off of walls in the middle of the night, dishes off of counters and Monistat 7 off of the bathroom sink.

That is not the sign of a normal dog.

I came home one day and she was wearing my underwear, her neck through the waistband and her front paws through each of the legs.

She barks at anything, but her most bitter enemies include paper, wind, clouds and bugs, and she hates them exceedingly at night. As a result, my husband and I have found ourselves shamefully throwing things at her should she nap during the day in an effort to keep her awake, simply to ensure ourselves a decent night's sleep.

It wasn't just my husband and me that suffered under Bella's reign of terror. Chigger, our other dog, a sweet, lovable older Labrador that we suspect is either brain damaged by the sun or the best dog in the world, has been used by Bella as a catapult, a trampoline and most predominately, a victim. As a result, Chig has taken to simply hiding out, and with today's date, we haven't seen her for nearly four months. We suspect, however, that she is still somewhere in the house because we haven't smelled a decomposing body, but then again, it's entirely possible that Bella ate her.

We don't believe Bella is a dog, but a secret government experiment. She owns the ability to zoom out of the house if I open the door a mere inch, then proceeds to run around in laps as if she was a calf with a branding iron positioned at her haunch. Honestly, I'm the last one who should be chasing a dingo out in my front yard. I'm so out of shape that if I try to exert myself my doing something physical like chew and walk at the same, I feel my left arm go numb, so I know not to push my luck.

But last week, as I went to check the mail, Bella got out and shot across the street, then back to our side, then back across. I stood on the porch and called to her sternly, but she was having none of it. She teased me, coming close enough for me to almost grab her when she would shoot out of range again and dart back across the street. Then, out of the corner of my eye, I saw flash of silver from the grill of a car that was racing down the road, headed right for us.

I had no choice.

I ran like the Six Million Dollar Woman and sprinted across the street, making as much noise except that it wasn't the sound of bionics in the background, it was my bones crushing together and my tonnage heaving up and down. I zeroed in on Bella, and, in a maneuver than can be officially classified as a miracle, I leapt off the ground and flung myself at my dog, landing on her at the same time the car whooshed by.

I laid there with Bella for a moment, trying to catch my breath at the same time that I felt my left arm start to tingle, and then, suddenly, I felt something bite into my thigh.

NO PEANUTS FOR YOU

"It's all strategy," I explained to my sister as we waited to board our plane. "I've booked us in row 17, which means we should be the first group to board after first class and the old people. Are you sure you're ready for this?"

My sister nodded.

"Now," I continued, "When they call for the rows 16 and higher, I want you to leap from your sprinter's position and run, with your elbows out, moving them like fins and blocking anyone who is trying to get ahead of you, until you hand the lady your boarding pass. Honestly, if it was up to me, I'd run the whole way to my seat, but that makes them think that you're carrying explosives on board and then it turns into this big mess."

"Tell me again why I have to run," my sister said as we moved forward in line.

I sighed. "Because of the limited and microscopic abundance of overhead compartment space," I tried to teach her. "Once, a couple with a baby, a car seat and a stroller got on ahead of me and I had to sit on my backpack the whole way to Chicago or the stewardess would have made me check it."

"And we didn't check our bags because...." my sister trailed off.

"Because I don't want to wear the same pair of underwear for seven days in a row on our vacation to Portland after our bags have been picked off my renegade luggage handlers," I explained. "There's only so many times you can turn underwear inside out before it begins to graft with your skin. Never again. Besides, my roll-on is very expensive and the handlers will see that as a form of wealth and think there's rubies inside instead of understanding that I bought it at T.J. Maxx for 75 percent off retail cost. It's got leather tags, you know. Although your luggage looks safe. I doubt anyone would take the time to mess with that. Isn't that the free bag you got after you bought make-up?"

My sister threw me a look.

"It's very nice for something that didn't cost you any money," I said as I heard my mother's voice come out of my mouth. "The good news is that I checked with the airline this morning, and there's no one sitting in front of us! We'll have leg space!"

"I certainly hope I get to enjoy that," my sister responded. "Maybe they don't even let my kind on a plane, you know with all of my possessions tied in a rag and attached to a pole and all."

"Look!" I shouted as I grabbed my roll-on. "The boarding pass lady just took position! Hurry! We've got to get a good spot! Strategy!"

We took our places in line as first class began to board, and as soon as the announcement came, my sister sped ahead with the brute force of an Olympic athlete on really good drugs. She scurried through the line with the agility of a woodland animal eluding a predator.

As I started to take off, however, the wheels of my roll-on locked and stopped, breaking my stride with a stumble. As I fumbled to regain my position, I looped another lady's duffel bag handle over my foot, and was prepared to take it with me had she not started to tug on it. I looked up in time to see my sister sprint onto the plane, her elbows still flapping as everyone else from rows 16 and up followed her.

When I finally got to my seat, my sister was reading a magazine and every overhead compartment was full. As I tried to carefully drape my skirt over my roll-on beneath me, a stewardess walked by and gave me a funny look.

"You're going to have to check the suitcase you're sitting on," she sighed, shaking her finger at me. "Your head is touching the ceiling, and for your information, I looked you up after last time. You are not the biggest giant woman in the world. Your feet aren't even touching the floor."

I handed over my luggage reluctantly. "You're going to be the first person served when I need someone to pay for skin grafts!" I said snidely.

"No peanuts for you!" she retorted.

As soon as the plane took off, the seat in front of me suddenly shot back, eliminating every inch of my comfort space. I gasped as I looked at my sister, who was lounging in her seat like she was on a cruise.

I was making faces at the unexpected passenger in front of me and kicking the back of his seat when his wrinkled, shaky arm, sheathed in skin as thin as paper, reached up and tried to flag down a flight attendant as his breathing rattled.

"I think he needs help!" my sister whispered. "Maybe he's sick!"

The thought of sitting behind a corpse all the way to Portland certainly didn't fit in with my vacation plans, so despite my hatred for the space stealer, I sprung into action.

"Help! Help!" I shouted. "Stewardess!"

The wrinkled arm gave one last shake, and finally collapsed.

"Sir, are you all right?" I said sitting forward, sticking my head between the seats. "Are you dead?"

The old man turned his head and looked at me. "What?" he said, giving me a dirty look. "Are you the one who keeps kicking me?"

"No," I continued. "That's CPR from behind."

"I was testing my air vent, you idiot," he answered. "And stop kicking me!"

As I sat back into the two inches of my traveling area, I heard him utter one word.

"Strategy."

What happens when you hit pause at the right moment before watching a show on Amazon.

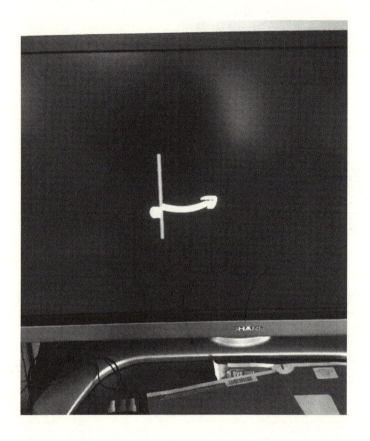

Brave Girl

I'm sitting in my car, on a stretch of I-10 that snaked past Casa Grande 16 miles ago.

It's dark, it's raining, the wind is blowing hard enough to rock my car from side to side like a bulimic trying to trick the last Whopper out of the carton. I've been here for an hour. It's 7:36 p.m., and there's enough of a line of other cars ahead of me that I can't see more than a couple hundred feet. I know this: In the hour that I've been here, I haven't moved an inch since I skidded to a squealing stop before the sun went down.

I pick up my cell phone that I use for special moments such as this. I'm sure my husband isn't panicked, but I dial the number anyway, right before the green lights on it flicker on and off, no service. Do not panic, I tell myself, there is nothing to panic about. I breathe in and slowly out several times. I'm hungry.

Be brave, a little voice whispers to me. You can do this. Don't start eating your fingers yet. Go for the butt first. The Donner party could have lived through the whole winter off that thing.

Being brave is something I haven't done since I quit drinking a zillion years ago. My brave heart days came to a sudden halt when I found myself laying in the dirt one night, my head cracked open by a metal rail of the railroad tracks. My skirt blew up over my head in an obvious act of redemption for prying the ashtrays out of the door of a cab with a butter knife earlier that night.

On I-10 an hour later, the car in front of me suddenly jerks forward and I see a trail of red brake lights ahead start to pop on. We're moving, I think happily, there's a detour. After two hours, they've finally made a detour and I can go home. Inch by inch, I crawl forward, following the trooper who's waving the flares. My heart jumps and my blood begins to rush, I'm 23 miles out of Phoenix, which means I'll be home by nine.

The trooper directs me to the left, and I follow the other cars through the dirt median, where we are forced to go left again, and, without any choice, back toward Casa Grande. What am I supposed to do in Casa Grande, I think angrily, the outlet malls are closing NOW.

I take the first exit, confident that I can find the access road and get back on a road to Phoenix. I follow about 10 other cars who have taken the exit, and I trail behind, making the turn onto the access road, the gold mine, that we have found. I know we've got to be on the right track judging by all of the headlights coming the opposite way, even though I recall the access road being a one-lane stretch.

Ten miles after I turned on this road, the red lights in front of me have disappeared. Only the oncoming traffic shows any other life, but I keep going, and going and going, until my car flies off asphalt and starts bumping along a dirt road.

I remember the access road being paved.

I'm lost. Somewhere in Southern Arizona, in the midst of a torrential rainstorm, at 10 p.m., I am lost. I try the cell phone again. No service.

I realize that the cars coming toward me were the cars I was following, only after a U-turn. I flip the car, sit for a moment and contemplate my options. I could bawl like a baby. I could spread open the car shade that my father bought me that screams "CALL POLICE" and wait until morning when a farmer finds me. I could light all the trash from my car on fire and wait until help came.

I hear that little whisper again, only this time it's louder, almost screaming at me.

Weren't you the one who climbed onto the roof of the Monte Vista and found an open window when you locked the keys in your room?

Yes, I answer, but I was drunk and I left my cigarettes in there.

Weren't you the one who made the first move on the guy that you eventually married?

Yes, but I was drunk and it was dark.

Hey! Weren't you the one who announced to the world that "The English Patient" sucked?

No, I pause, that was Elaine from Seinfeld.

WELL THEN DO SOMETHING BRAVE, the voice sputters. GET ON THAT ROAD AND FIND YOUR WAY HOME, LASSIE!!

I put my foot on the accelerator and get back on the road, get back on the interstate and drive determined to get home. Soon, another detour pops up and I find out I'm going to Florence, toward the state prison, with a thousand other cars ahead of me, and at five miles an hour, we all creep equally toward Phoenix. It's a long ride, and eventually, I've smoked a pack of cigarettes. By 11:30, I reach the outskirts of Chandler, find access back to I-10 and am flying toward downtown.

At midnight, I pull in front of my house.

I am tired. I'm still hungry, I smell like an ashtray and I have to go to the bathroom. My husband meets me on the porch, picks up my suitcase and looks at me.

"You're so brave," he says. "even though you were mostly in the dark."

I got searched again at the airport. The TSA *guy opened my luggage. And then this happened.*

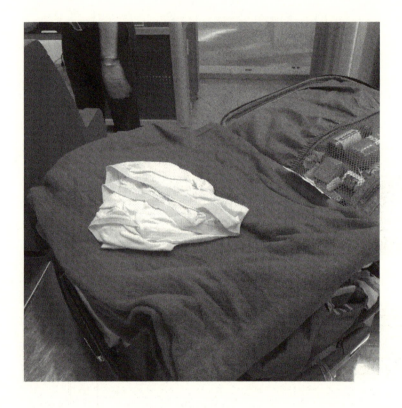

YOU COUNT

I am being watched.

Armed with clipboards, pens and beady little spy eyes, they know when I'm home, at work or hiding from them in the bathroom, and they camouflage themselves on the porch until I think the coast is clear.

They know almost everything about me, and what they don't know, they're bound and determined to find out.

I am being stalked by the Census people.

I will be honest and admit that I did not return my Census form on time through the mail, mainly because I cleaned my house and lost it. When I finally found it, I learned that my hell hound of a dog had mistaken it for a burglar or violation from the neighborhood association and had put it through the shredder we call her jaw.

"That's right, Census Bureau," I thought. "The dog ate my homework. How do you like that!"

Not very much, it turned out.

The Census Bureau did not send me another pleasant reminder in the mail as I had hoped; they sent Marie.

Apparently, Marie had been watching me for a while. She left notes on my door asking me to call her at home. That, to me, sounded weird, and reminded me of the time many years ago that a fat bass player from a punk band used to follow me around every night and left dirty napkins on my car, asking if I would call him because he wanted to "pluck my strings." I finally got rid of him one night when he locked himself around my leg and refused to let me get in my car. I shook him loose with the words, "Go home, little doggie," to which he looked up at me and replied, "You have a big butt and you're only pretty when I'm drunk!"

Now, the last thing I wanted to do was have to beat Marie off of my leg with a stick, so I didn't call her back. But that certainly wasn't going to stop her. Because of her spying, Marie knew the most appropriate time to strike. At the exact moment that I stepped out of the shower, the phone rang and a Fed Ex guy needed my signature for a package, Marie staged her attack and jumped up on the porch.

"How many people live in this house?" she asked as she forced herself in front of the Fed Ex guy. "Does he live here? Is that towel Egyptian cotton or domestic? How many towels do you have? Who's on the phone? Do they live here and if so, has it been since April 1st?"

"I'm sorry," I said as I tried to sign the package receipt and hold the towel tight up against all parts of me that I hadn't shaved. "Can you come back some other time?"

And so she did.

This time she lurked outside until the swamp cooler belched loudly, began shooting hundreds of gallons of water off my roof and the hell hound shot out the door as soon as I opened it.

"PICK ONE: WHITE, AFRICAN-AMERICAN, HISPANIC AMERICAN OR ASIAN/PACIFIC ISLANDER AMERICAN!!" she shouted over the torrent of water as I tried to find the shut-off valve in my front yard.

"NONE OF THE ABOVE!" I shouted back. "HOW ABOUT IRATE AMERICAN WITH CRAPPY HOMEOWNER'S INSURANCE AND A TENDANCY TO EXACT HER ANGER ON NEAREST PERSON WITHIN HITTING DISTANCE NAMED MARIE? DO YOU HAVE A CATEGORY FOR THAT? MAYBE YOU COULD COME BACK?"

The next time Marie came calling, she brought a chair, a tent and enough beef jerky to last for weeks. I let her make camp for several days until I saw her haul out a huge boom box, point it toward my bedroom and toss a Van Halen CD in it.

"Little pig, little pig, let me in," she taunted from her beach chair. "Or 'Hot For Teacher' will soon begin!"

"OKAY, okay!" I shouted as came out, waving a pair of white panties. "What do you want?"

Marie scrambled over with her clipboard. "Are you married?" she asked.

"I know! I can't believe it, either!" I said excitedly.

"What kind of fuel heats your house?" she asked.

"Good old fashioned hate," I replied.

"Have you even been laid off?" she questioned.

"You don't have enough beef jerky for me to answer that question," I answered.

"Do you sell agricultural products?" she queried.

"No, but I had boyfriends that did," I nodded.

"Is an occupant of this house incarcerated?" she posed.

"You government people never stop, do you!" I pouted. "I have PAID my debt! I only *watered* those plants!"

"Your annual income?" she continued.

I paused, then I smiled. "Um, a million dollars," I lied. "I'm a very important...worker. I'm beginning to like the census!"

"And your age?" she prodded.

"33!" I lied again. "No! I'm 24! THAT was a very good year, well, except for the probation part. You know, I think I LOVE the census! Do you need my weight, too? It's 108!"

"I see you're dyslexic, too, huh?" she said, checking another box. "Okay. We're all done."

I was a little shocked.

"Are you sure?" I asked. "Because there's so much more to know. I mean, we've just barely cracked the door here. Don't you want to know where I went to college? I went to UCHarvard. I can do a backbend. But only when I'm on pain pills. And sometimes, sometimes, I know things before they happen. Like the you and Van Halen? I had a feeling you were a fan. Sometimes, it's scary to be psychic."

"I'm sorry," Marie said. "I have a diabetic man that I need to ambush. I just discovered a hedge that I might be able to leap and latch on to his scooter from. His scooter goes very fast. He's eluded me for weeks. Threatened to throw his pee on me."

I nodded and pursed my lips. "Smart," I nodded. "Brilliant tactic."

"So I'll see you in four years?" Marie said as she stepped off the porch.

"Yep," I said. "Unless I get a scooter and a Thirstbuster full of urine by then.

THE VOICES

Could it be true?

Was I really hearing voices?

I was dialing my friend Robert's phone number when I heard it the first time. It was always the same woman's voice, slow, low, and barely audible.

But just as soon as it started, the voice suddenly stopped, and Robert answered his phone. He was the only person I know who could get me out of my computer mess, because he is so technologically capable that he once built a kitchen clock out of Nixie tubes. I didn't know what they were, either, but to me, that just proves how smart he is.

I've heard of urban legends in which people buy a computer, take it out of the box, plug it in and it actually works.

Things like that just do not happen.

Especially not to ME.

No, no, that's not the way things work in my world. I'm never surprised when I buy something new, I plug it in and it shorts out my electricity, is missing a part or suddenly bursts into flames and melts other appliances around it as well.

So, really, how could I have been shocked when I unpacked my new computer and spent four hours setting it up, only to discover that as a couple, we were not hitting it off?

It stared at me with a blank screen, teased me several times with a faint flicker, and then gently eased back into it's technology coma. That's when I got up and called Robert.

He heard my cry and was at my door in an hour.

"Oh yes," he said, probing and poking where all the wires are attached to the monitor. "I can see the problem here. At this point, you have two alternatives: Send the computer back, or learn how to push the ON button."

The next day, I settled down and went to work. I pushed "Print," only to have my happy new computer inform me that it was going to be utterly, utterly impossible.

I was in the kitchen dialing Robert's number when I heard her—the Voice—speak to me again.

It was definitely not my neighbor. I stopped and tried to make out the words, but all I could make out was the word "serve."

This is impossible, I thought. There has to be an explanation, a rational one like my dog yawning, or maybe she has some bad gas.

In an hour, Robert was poking at the wires again when he mentioned, "The printer only works when you plug it into the hard drive. You plugged the printer back into itself. It's not a worm, you know."

Much later that night, I was getting ready for bed. As I brushed my teeth, the Voice came to me again.

"Warning," she said to me in a mumble I could barely understand. "Serve the apple!"

This time, I totally freaked out. Oh my God, I thought to myself. Am I going crazy? Serve the apple? Is it like Son of Sam, but only with a fruit? Son of Red Delicious? Am I possessed? Am I going to start killing people on the advice from a member of one of the four basic food groups?

Then I heard her speak again: "Serve and apple. Respond."

This voice was there. I was NOT imagining it. I heard it. I HEARD it.

I couldn't sleep at all that night. I didn't understand what it wanted me to do, and I couldn't tell my husband. He's just looking for an excuse. I decided that the voice wasn't nasty, so it probably wasn't a demon, and since it was a lady's voice, I deducted that it pretty much had to be the Virgin Mary. But I had already decided it would be smart not to say anything because I saw what happened when someone thought they saw Jesus' face on a dirty wall someplace near Nogales. People flocked from all around and *they brought tents*. The last thing I need is a yard full of people yelling for me to heal them and asking to use my bathroom. I have to take six Motrin just to get rid of my own headache.

The next morning, I even felt holier. I felt chosen, and I kind of looked forward to what the Mother of God had to say to me next, unless it was "You could be so pretty if you just lost some weight."

As soon as I sat down to work, though, I ran quickly from a good mood into a bad one when my computer totally and completely crashed again.

"Robert," I said into the phone.

"I'll be right there," he answered.

Then I looked at the computer, and I got really, really mad. Nothing works for me. Nothing, *ever*. It was really unfair. Stupid thing. I hate it. I hate it. I HATE IT.

And, before I even knew what I was doing, I had reached out and smacked the screen with my very own hand.

"That's not very saintly," a nosybody voice in my head said. "I'm telling the Virgin Mary!"

When Robert arrived, he sat at the computer, looked at it curiously and then looked at me.

"Have you been hurting this computer?" he asked me, point blank. "Have you been messing with it on purpose?"

"What?" I replied. "No, I haven't been hurting it! It hates me! It's been hurting me!"

"You know, I suspected a while ago that something wasn't right here," he said sharply. "You had all of these problems with it, and I'd come over and fix them every time. But now, I see your hand print on the screen, and you know what I think? I think you like the attention you get when your computer's broken. In fact, I think you break it on purpose. And that hand print is the proof I've been waiting for!"

"Robert——" I started.

"Oh, no!" he said standing up. "You're sick! It's Munchausen Syndrome by proxy, I've seen your kind before! I'm calling CPS! Computer Protective Services, sister!"

"Robert, that is ridiculous!" I said adamantly, stamping my foot. "Do you think the Virgin Mary would talk to someone that abuses her very own computer? I'm holy! I'm going to be serving the holy apple, or something like that. She told me herself!"

"Serving the apple?" Robert said, unbelievingly. "So what's she look like? Hmmm?"

"I've never seen her..." I stammered. "But I hear her all the time!"

"Oh yeah?" he said, staring at me. "Does she sound like...this?"

And then he reached over, pushed three keys.

A voice suddenly popped up.

"Warning! The server is not connected to the Apple remote access and does not respond," my computer said.

"Oh my God," I said. "You mean I hit the Virgin Mary?"

Stopped and smelled one of my roses. Sucked a petal up my nostril. Reflexively shot it back out but instead saw a giant aphid land on the flower. Clearly not the first time this has happened. To either of us.

CONTAGIOUS

I had a feeling I was going to get it.

As soon as he walked through the door with his hand at his throat, his face wearing the Sick Man look, I had suspected I was a goner.

Of course, it made sense. With a long-awaited vacation only five days away, it was just a given that somehow, some way, something was going to knock me full of cootie germs and I would be boarding that plane clutching multiple bottles of Afrin and a ream of Kleenex.

My husband you see, works at an office that doubles as a germ factory. The CDC currently gives his office the same rating as a daycare center on the contamination scale, causing me to caution him aloud, "If you see anything that you think is chocolate but isn't in its' original packaging, DON'T touch it and immediately call your supervisor." I suspected for a while that he might have been an undercover government scientist conducting biohazard research because we both get sick roughly once a month, and but then I realized that Africa has better medical coverage than we do with our HMO and he only gets four holidays off a year. Even spies get more vacation time.

The Sick Out routinely begins with a subtle complaint on his part (i.e.: aches and pains; a small, yet painful, pustule; the conjecture that the lining of his small intestines may have just fallen out of his body), and within three days, we're both stumbling around the house like junkies, hopped up on Theraflu and searching the carpet for the last Sudafed with our red, leaky eyes.

So when he walked through the front door last Thursday clutching his neck, my survival instincts kicked in and I immediately covered my mouth. This time, I wasn't going to take it. This time, I was fighting back.

"Oh no you don't!" I yelled, running behind a chair. "We're going on vacation in five days and you are NOT going to get me sick again!"

"I'm all hot and sweaty, I can't swallow and I'm seeing some pretty scary things," he said with imploring eyes. "On the way home, I saw Tom Selleck kissing Rosie O'Donnell in the back of a red El Camino. It wasn't real, was it?"

"I'll tell you what is real," I said, backing up into the next room. "You're not coming any closer until I scrub you with a wire brush and spray you down with Lysol!"

"I am not a toilet!" he cried hoarsely. "I'm human!"

"Why can't you bring Post-It notes and paper clips home from work like everyone else?" I cried. "Why does it have to be plagues and pestilence?"

"I just wanna go to bed," he said weakly as he shuffled past me.

"No no no"! I shouted, blocking his path. "You're not contaminating MY room, you Pox Peddler! Are you crazy? There are Ralph Lauren sheets in there! If you lay down, I'll have to burn them!"

"Well, then what do you want me to do?" my husband said, turning toward me, his chapped, red nostrils flaring, his puffy, swollen upper lip quivering. "Should I sleep in my car? Is that what you want?"

"Okay, you can sleep in the bed," I said very sternly. "But only under one condition: DON'T BREATHE ON ME. Sleep with your back toward me. And no farts. You breach this contract and I will evict you, understood?"

"Fine," he said as he slipped under the covers.

When I went to bed later that night, I made sure that he had kept his bargain and was shooting his germ warfare in the other direction. Fifteen minutes later, however, I woke up to something growling in my ear. When I turned over, there it was. A full, open-mouthed, hot, air jet-stream of disease and misery blowing out of my husband's mouth like a hand-held Vornado, huffing so hard it was moving my hair.

Hey, Osama bin Laden, I said as shook him awake. This love has boundaries, you know! Take your cholera to the couch, buddy!

He grumbled loudly as he rambled down the hallway, a pillow tucked under his arm.

"HEY!" I shouted after him. "I said no farts!"

The next morning, I woke up and decided that we desperately needed to establish a set of rules to govern our household as my husband climbed further up the corporate ladder of illness.

Rule 1: Should he have a sore throat, he shouldn't come home and BREATHE ON ME.

Rule 2: Should he have a stuffy nose, he shouldn't come home and BREATHE ON ME.

Rule 3: Should he feel a little cold and clammy, he shouldn't come home and BREATHE ON ME.

Rule 4: Should he feel a tightness in his chest and a numbness in his left arm, he can breathe on me, but only for a little bit until he shows me where the insurance policy is.

Rule 5: From this moment on, Bean-o goes on absolutely everything the man eats from sun up to sundown, and I mean *everything*.

I went to inform him of these new rules, but the couch was empty save for two pillows that vaguely looked like him.

I eventually found him in his study, wedged into the two-foot space in between an amplifier and his desk on a folded up blanket, sleeping there like a little dog.

"It's your duty as the wife to heal me," he groaned.

"It's your duty as a husband not to get me sick right before I go on vacation," I insisted, helping him up. "But I guess your commitments as Patient Zero override that."

"You're blaming the wrong source," he informed me as he blew his nose. "I didn't mean to get sick."

"Yeah, well, tell that to our neighbors," I mentioned. "One of them painted a black X on the front door and the rest of the villagers are ready to brick us in our own house! My vacation will be ruined!"

"Don't worry," my husband said, waving his hand. "Your incubation period is almost over. In about four days, the blisters on your eyelids will pop, you'll have sloughed off your first three layers of skin, your lizard tongue will retract and you'll be on the road to recovery and on that plane. Simple as that."

I just stared at him.

"Oh, did I tell you at work we switched to a PPO?" he added.

THE FIRST DAY

There he was, dressed in his favorite striped T-shirt, his little cargo shorts and his backpack slung over one shoulder.

"Okay," my husband said as he took the steps down the front porch. "I'm going to school now."

And then, he turned around once, looked back toward home, at me standing in the doorway, and waved good-bye. He was off for his first day.

"Bye," he said again, still looking back.

It was killing me. Ripping my black little stone heart right in two.

Well, not really. Honestly, I couldn't wait for him to get out of the house.

You see, ever since my husband changed his schedule at work to accommodate his classes at ASU, he's been home during the day. Every day. And that's the same 'every day' when I'm trying to work and get stuff done.

So all summer long, I waited impatiently for the first day of school to hurry up and get there, and it had finally arrived. As a wife, I saw it as my duty to make sure that it was a flawless experience for him

The reason I was preparing him was because I didn't want him coming back. I don't mean *ever*, I just mean in the when it's light outside. Having both of us home when I was supposed to be at my most productive wasn't exactly working out.

Being that he had signed up for Spanish this semester, he decided a great way to get a healthy head start would be to watch Spanish soap operas in the morning to get a firm 'grasp' of the language.

I'd be in my office, typing away, when I'd hear him make a deep sigh and slap his knee.

"What is Miguel thinking?" I'd hear him say to himself. "He has a perfectly good family, a nice home, kids, and he's throwing it all away for that *promiscuo* An-hell! What an *idioto*! Can't you *see*, Miguel? She's bad! She's a bad, *bad* senorita!"

"Anthill and Miguel can't hear you," I yelled back. "But I can. And I'm WORKING."

"It's An-hell, honey," he tried to explain. "An-hell, or, I guess to a gringa like you, it's just plain Angel."

"I'd be rapidly approaching a deadline when he'd poke his head around the corner, rub his stomach and say, "I'm hungry. Want to get something to eat?"

"Macaroni and cheese in the cupboard," I'd respond without looking up. "But if I catch you taking stuff from the Year 2000 stockpile again, I'm going to stop WORKING and kill you."

"It was only one Cup of Noodles!" he'd argue.

"I'll remind you of that on January 11th, when you're cold, hungry and bored because you can't watch Spanish TV since the world has come to a grinding halt," I replied. "And we've just eaten the last jar of the Vienna sausages and canned creamed corn."

I'd be in the bathroom when he'd knock on the door and sorrowfully ask, "Can I come in? I'm lonely."

"I'm WORKING!" I'd yell.

I'd be trying to figure out a punchline when he'd come into the office, stand behind me, dishevel my hair and cry playfully, "Honey! I have a great idea! Let's go to the movies!"

"You know," I finally said one day. "I would love to go to the movies. I really would. But I can't go to the movies, and I can't because I'm WORKING. How would you like it if I came to your work and asked you to go to the movies? That would be torture, wouldn't it?"

He hung his head and nodded as he shuffled out of the room.

So as the first day of school came closer, I decided to prep my husband for any emergencies that might pop up and cause him to come running home.

"Your classes are in the Social Sciences building," I said, pointing it out on a map. "Helpful hint here: On the second floor, there's a clean, little-known bathroom that hardly anyone uses. *You know.* In case of a surprise attack."

"Now," I cautioned. "If you get lost, don't panic. Ask an adult to point you to a big map. They're all over the place."

He just stared at me.

"Do you have anyone to eat lunch with?"

"If your shoes become untied, don't get excited. Just ask your teacher for help."

"Guess what? They have a McDonald's there! You *like* that!"

"If you make a friend, maybe we can have a camp-out in the backyard this weekend!"

I covered as much terrain as I could, taught him everything I knew about ASU. As I watched him walk down the front steps of our porch, I knew the rest was up to him.

After I waved good-bye, I went back inside, shuffled into my office and sat in front of the computer.

Sure was quiet.

Yep.

Just the way I like it.

I went to work, and started typing.

It was really quiet.

What a luxury, I thought to myself. Now this is quiet!

I liked the quiet, I really did, but turned on Spanish TV just for some background noise. Alma, Miguel's wife, had caught him with Anthill and was trying to get both of them to eat some poison taffy she had just made.

I went back to work, but something felt wrong. It felt different.

It just didn't feel right.

Suddenly I realized what it was. I was lonely.

Before I knew it, I was in the car, driving at furious speeds, switching from one lane to the next like a Road Rager.

I was there in fifteen minutes.

I ran up the steps, taking two at a time, and scurried down the long, sterile hall.

I found the right door, and held up my note against the large glass window in it.

"Great idea!" the note said. "Want to go to the movies, honey?"

TRIPLE-WIDE COUNTRY

We've all heard the standard joke about country music—If you play a country song backwards, the singer gets his job back, his woman comes home and his dog springs back to life. Well, that's the way it used to be.

I know a little about country music. I've wailed to Patsy Cline's "Crazy" in my car until one particularly sour note popped out a chip of glass on my rearview mirror. I know that Hank Williams eventually pickled himself to death in the back seat of a convertible on a cold New Year's Eve. When I was a little kid, my mom would snap off the radio when Loretta Lynn's "The Pill" or "Don't Come Home a Drinkin' With Lovin' On Your Mind" soared across the dial, and I saw Urban Cowboy on the big screen when it first came out and immediately went to Lerner's to buy a pair of Sassoon jeans with the saddle-stitched butt.

Admittedly, I'm not an enthusiast about today's country music, however; I'll confess that I almost pushed my mother to the ground at my wedding when she suggested that we line-dance to Achy Breaky Heart and got a little angry when I heard that Garth Brooks was billed as "The World's Greatest Performer" when the lid of Frankie's casket hadn't been closed yet. The nerve.

But I hadn't really begun to understand the mass market appeal of country music until I saw a television biography of Patsy Cline several weeks ago and an abundance of supermodels kept popping up, professing how the legendary country singer had influenced their careers.

"That's stupid," I remarked to my husband. "How in the world can Patsy Cline influence a pelvic thrust and a confused gaze in a Victoria's Secret commercial?"

"I don't think those are models," he answered. "I think they're all country singers."

I was stunned. "Those girls all had their own teeth," I said in amazement. "And they weren't even bucked. People don't walk out of the backwoods of Appalachia looking like that! I bet not a one of them have ever eaten possum!"

This event prompted me to take a peek at the country music video channel, and after an hour, it got to the point that I couldn't tell one hillbilly vixen from the next. Only one of them shot their video in a mobile home, because all of the rest of the sirens were too busy frolicking on the beach or rolling around on the floor in what looked like Czar Nicholas' Winter Palace, clothed in either just a towel or sequined evening gowns. This isn't country, I thought to myself. Minnie Pearl wore the same gingham dress for fifty years, never once entertained the thought of frosted lipstick and wouldn't dream about pounding on her cowbell in a robe with the neckline exposed down to her first belly roll. Country music today doesn't seem to be much more than silicone pop music with an extended pronunciation of every "r."

Now, far be it for me to say that Loretta, Patsy or Dolly aren't attractive gals, but they aren't Playboy material. In today's market, would any of their talents even have been noticed? I have to wonder. I can clearly see the image of a country music exec with his Justins propped up on his desk, screaming into a phone, "Yeah, yeah, yeah. So she can sing. How good does she look without a Wonderbra?"

Sure, the current leading ladies of country can belt out a tune, I won't argue with that. But it seems to me that country music was perhaps the last safe bastion of success based purely on talent, what the roots of country were fed with. It didn't used to matter what you looked like. You weren't supposed to be a sex symbol when wading through a wrenching ballad about your cheating husband. That no longer holds true. It's not good enough to have a pair of knockout lungs—singers have to have other knockout pairs to boot, and we're not talking feet. When did Hee-Haw become Baywatch? There just may be average-looking country entertainers, but they either have stand-ins or they're not allowed on TV. I sure didn't see them. It's not limited to women, either; a hearty portion of singing cowboys look more like Calvin Klein poster boys with goatees and carefully battered Stetsons. The only difference is that they go the extra mile and actually take their shirts off and then start lifting things.

It's a standard we expect, and demand, from pop culture, but country? Can a gorgeous yodeler in a 100 percent silk shirt and a personal trainer on the payroll honestly wail "Weary Blues From Waitin'" with the emotion required to carry that song off? I don't think so. It's a song that needs to be sung right by a man with bleeding gum disease, only has fourteen percent of his working liver left and who wraps electrical tape around the sole of his boot because he can't afford another pair. And he's got hemorrhoids, too. Someone that's seen real pain.

Well, there is some solace in this, I guess. Perhaps we can look forward to a remake of Urban Cowboy with Leonardo DiCaprio and Claudia Schiffer in the starring roles. Of course, they'd live in a triple-wide and drive a Hummer, but we just couldn't accept any less, could we? Maybe it all started when Roy Clark got hair plugs. I suppose when his life story is made into a mini-series, we'll finally get to see George Clooney strumming on a banjo.

Maybe it's all Roy's fault that if you play a country song backward today, the singer just gets dressed.

I had a terrible dream that my dad died from choking on tomato soup. It was awful. It also happened to be the day my sister Linda was going to get married. I was crying, and crying, and said, "Of course we're going to cancel the wedding," but my mother said, "Don't be ridiculous. We'll just push it back an hour. Everything's already been PAID FOR, Laurie!"

DAVEEEEED

He was really, really pink and he focused at me with his left eye as his right tried to follow.

"I used to date a guy that looked at me the very same way after he drank a quart of gin," I said to my mother as she stood next to me. "And he used to flail his arms just like this, too, when he didn't take his medicine!"

"You're ruining the moment," my mother said as she leaned in for a closer look. "He's 15 minutes old, Laurie. I don't think the first thing your new nephew needs to know about you is that you've dated every AA member in the Phoenix chapter."

I arrived at the hospital an hour before where my sister was having her labor induced, only to find her sitting up in bed, her hair done and make-up perfectly applied.

"Are you okay?" I asked when I saw her and noticed the contraction monitor needling off the charts.

"Oh, yeah, I'm fine, I'm on enough drugs to could knock a horse on it's rear," she said with a smile as the needle screamed red ink louder. "But I'd feel a lot better if I could read that People magazine that I brought with me. *It's the best and worst dressed issue*!"

"I'm almost done with it," her husband said from the chair next to her bed. "I'm just trying to figure out how Jennifer Lopez kept that dress...attached."

"Where's Mom?" I asked, noticing that we were the only people in the room, and knowing how badly my mother wanted to be there.

"She's watching Nicholas with Dad," my sister said, referring to her three-year old son.

"Oh," I said, figuring this was a touchy spot. My mother had made no bones about informing all of us that she intended to be at the birth of the new baby, but my sister was having none of it.

"I'll tell you right now that this is not a ticket-holder's event," she said the week before during Sunday dinner. "This IS NOT a peep show, and my privates are not going on display for public viewing. I don't want people looking at places on me that I don't even look at myself."

"What about the nurses? They'll see your who-see-what-sis," my mother said, trying to plead her case with what looked like tears in her eyes.

"I don't have to sit across from the nurse when I'm eating dinner when she says, 'How's the ham? I've seen your who-see-what-sis. Pass the gravy,'" my sister snapped. "Besides, I'm thinking about wearing a mask at the hospital in case I run into one of them later when I'm at the mall."

"I have a Monica Lewinsky mask," I offered.

"I think I may go as Jennifer Lopez," my sister replied. "She doesn't seem to care if the whole world sees her naughty bits, not just the President."

"Mommy," my nephew Nicholas interjected, "You could wear my elephant costume when baby brother comes. And Aunt Laurie could wear my Buzz Lightyear costume when her baby comes."

"Oh, I'm not having a baby, but thank you," I said with a giggle.

Nicholas paused, looking puzzled. "But you have the same belly as Mommy," he finally said.

Admittedly, in a comparison between the girth of the my and my sister's bellies, there wasn't much discrepancy, but I tried to stay calm. "There's no baby in here," I said, pointing to my paunch. "There's just Twinkies and Pepsi. And I keep brownies and ice cream in my bum."

He looked at me and sighed. "Crazy Aunt Laurie," he said, twirling a circle with his finger at his head.

"Who taught him that!" I demanded, but they all looked away.

"I bet Aunt Laurie will let me be there when *her* Twinkie is born," my mother said with a sly grin.

"If that's what you want, you got it, Mom," I said. "In fact, I just had another contraction and I feel like I have to push. Meet you in the potty!"

Now in her hospital bed a week later, my sister was tearing the eyes and mouth out of the photo of Jennifer Lopez when she suddenly looked up and said, "I think I have to push."

"Hold on," the nurse advised her. "The doctor isn't here yet."

"Out!" my sister said as she pointed to me, and, understanding her rules, I obliged.

I hadn't been in the waiting room for more than three minutes when my Mom popped up.

"I can't find your sister's room," she said in a panic, breathing hard. "I can't find the room!"

Ah, an undercover raid, I thought to myself, my mother's secret plan all along.

"You're smooth, Mom," I complimented her. "Sneak attacks have always been your special talent. Remember when you read my diary and I wrote that the only reason you had me was so you'd have a slave to empty the dishwasher?"

"I'm not sneaking!" my mother said in protest. "Your sister called me this morning and said I could come!"

"Oh," I said, understanding. "Yeah, she's on more drugs than Robert Downey, Jr."

Together, we raced down the hall just in time to hear a nurse outside my sister's room scream, "We need help in here! WE NEED SOME HELP NOW!"

My mother nearly knocked the nurse over as she pushed her way into the room and I followed. She quickly ripped the curtain aside and stood there as I remained behind, and I heard my mother gasp.

Through a break in the curtain, I saw a little body covered in what looked like marshmallow fluff pass behind my sister's knee. I could see little arms moving, hands balled up in a tiny fist.

And then I heard a cry.

"It's a fat little boy," I heard the doctor say.

"These drugs are great," I heard my sister say. "Can I buy them at Walgreen's?"

"Here's your baby," the nurse said, holding him up for my sister to see.

"So that's the foot that's been lodged between my ribs and my kidneys for the last three months," my sister said.

I stepped out from behind the curtain when I got the "all clear" sign, and when I sat down in the chair, the nurse brought the now pink marshmallow fluff baby over and let me hold him.

"Hi," I said as his eyes kept trying to focus. "I'm Crazy Aunt Laurie." Then a felt a little "POOT!" come from the bottom of the blanket. "Twinkies already, huh? "I said. "You're my kind of guy."

EL DIABLO

For about a month, my husband had retreated into his little man, cave, shutting the door behind and then remaining there for hours. Initially I thought that perhaps he was reading an emotional novel and didn't want me to see his tears, or was simply plotting my murder.

But soon, baffling, loud noises began emanating from his room, like womanly moaning that was soon were followed by grunts of "Uh! Ahhhhh! Uh! Ahhhhh! Uh! Ahhhhh!" Then came the voices, as that of a middle-aged Scottish man asking, "Hullo there! Whut ca I du fer ya?" With a chill that began winding slowly up my spine, I arrived upon a couple of conclusions: 1) My husband's office was a portal for exotic and chatty spirits from the netherworld, which was good because I had encouraged him to make new friends; 2) He had found a fabled and very rare Leprechaun or troll under a bridge and was now securing it in the Man Cave until he surprised me with it at Christmas; or 3) I would know the hit man my husband had hired because he would probably be wearing a skirt and no underpants.

One day, as the grunts and groans floated out into the hallway from behind the Man Cave door, I simply couldn't take it anymore, mainly because if there was a Leprechaun in there, I wanted to start playing with it right away. So I swung open the door quickly and caught my husband by surprise.

"Don't look at me!" he cried as he turned his head away from me. "I'm so...ashamed!"

"Oh my God!" I cried in horror when I saw the object in his right hand, which he was gripping tightly. "That's nearly obscene! Look at all of that testosterone! You're grabbing that mouse the way a woman clutches a new credit card!"

"Well, what do you expect me to do?" my husband snapped. "I'm at a very tense moment here! I just met the demon they call 'The Butcher'!"

In hindsight, I should have seen the signs--the distraction, the secrecy, the female wailing--but maybe I just didn't want to know. Maybe I didn't want to come to terms that the man I thought I was sharing my life with was having all of his needs filled by slaughtering hundreds of cartoon characters an hour. He had become a computer game addict, and his favorite fix was *Diablo*.

Apparently, I'm not the only *Diablo* widow around, I'm merely one of many. Once my husband's secret was out, our household became like those others with menfolk often yelping from their Diablo hideouts, "Hey! Who threw that fireball?", "How tough can sword-brandishing evil skeletons be when you all look like supermodels?" and "Say hello to my newest supernatural power, Holy Bolt, as well as an old favorite, The Firewall of Ultimate Agony, you angry mob of undead!"

But life in the Diablo world often overlapped in other areas, such as when my husband woke up from a nightmare in which 100 naked women marched toward him, only to stop and shoot fiery arrows at his head, and when a $400 electric bill was overdue, he told me he'd take care of it by deploying a fire bolt.

That sort of blurring the lines of reality was unsettling, but I was also sure that he'd get bored with the game eventually. That was until I realized that as long as there's fire, weapons and the occasional hope of spotting a scantily clad figure with hips, (even if she is trying to impale him with a javelin like a rotisserie chicken) a man will stay chained to that dream until the power company finally turns the lights out, despite the efforts of the aforementioned fire bolt.

I had no choice; I was going to have to send my old man to Diablo rehab. Honestly, there really is no such thing, but I decided to create my own prison by simply unplugging the computer, claiming it blew up when our power was restored as the result of a massive donation from my bank account that they call a deposit, and making my husband keep repeating the one part in rehab where addicts have to say they're sorry all the time.

It sounded good to me, but when I went into his office to rip the cord out of the wall, there my husband sat, fighting the undead as they pelted him with maces. Suddenly, in the corner of the screen, I saw something small and green scurry by.

"Hey, was that a Leprechaun?" I asked eagerly.

"I think it's an incubus with the powers of resurrection, but it is little, weird and green," he answered.

"Scoot over," I said adamantly, "and give me that mouse."

FOCUS ON FUN

To focus on fun or *not* to focus on fun. That was the question.

And, frankly speaking, I didn't have an answer.

You see, for the past several years when our birthdays rolled around, my best friend, Jamie, and I have taken a vacation to San Francisco. The tradition began when we jointly took a maturity quiz in a magazine and realized we qualified as adults when we both affirmatively replied to, "Have you recently vocalized, to yourself or to another, 'We, I should really have a doctor check that thing out.'"

We figured then that if our days of youth and bone density were quickly coming to an end, we'd better take advantage of the time we had left and travel. Thus, our trip, aptly named Focus on Fun, was born because after all, you can only depend on acne to make you look young for so long before the gray hair narcs you off.

But this year, admittedly, I felt a little skittish. And I didn't want to feel that way. I wanted to be able to stoutly demand that I was boarding that plane for Focus on Fun 2001, unafraid and determined. I had even choreographed scenarios in my head of lunging at the terrorist with a Vulcan grip and a swift kick where it counts. Then I throw the weeping, bruised evil doer to the ground and shout, "You tell Osama Yo Mama to bring it on with the chicks who simultaneously have acne, gray hair and suspicious moles, buddy! Because THAT is anger, Captain Cave, THAT IS ANGER!" Suddenly, I look down and am dressed in a denim jumpsuit unzipped to my sternum and behind me, Kate Jackson and Jaclyn Smith are ready to hand out free samples of Kickbutt Pie. Oh yeah, and my frosted, immaculately feathered hair ROCKS, making a majority of the other passengers visibly jealous. Now, despite the bravado of my Nick at Night mind, I was two weeks away from the date of our trip and still didn't have a plane ticket. Sure, I had been busy, or I didn't have the money, but truth be told I was stalling. Almost like if I waited long enough, I wouldn't have to decide at all.

And then Jamie called from her house in Los Angeles.

"Okay," she said. "What's the deal? Are we going or not? You haven't said a word about Focus on Fun 2001, and usually you're packed and at the airport by now, eating Cinnabons like a bear heading into hibernation."

"Well," I started, a bit shakily. "I'm not sure where I can even park at the airport anymore, it's confusing."

"Oh, come on," my best friend scoffed. "For me to fly out of LAX, I have to go through more security than either of Madonna's weddings then grant a camouflaged person holding a rifle permission to pat my paunch. Before, I never let anyone get that familiar with me without a ring and the correlating receipt first. I need a vacation and I am ready to FOCUS ON FUN!"

"Are you the least bit scared?" I offered hesitantly.

"*Scared?*" Jamie replied, almost in a yell. "Listen, I've got a freckle on my arm that's changing colors more frequently than a Rainbow Brite, and either the zipper on the back of my sweater got bent at the dry cleaner's or I now have a neck hump the size of a bagel. I ran out of fear before I even left the house this morning. I'm FOCUSING ON FUN!"

"There's only one way to settle this," I offered. "We'll take a vote."

"I vote to go," Jamie said. "It's our duty. The economy of our nation is in our hands. With all the shopping we'll do, Alan Greenspan will probably *raise* interest rates by the time we get home. How do you vote?"

"I was going to vote which ever way you did," I admitted meekly.

"Great!" Jamie said. "FOCUS ON FUN! Now, where do you think I can get a denim jumpsuit at?"

When I picked up my iPhone, for some reason, I had a screen saver of Mandy Patinkin. I thought my husband did it, so I started to laugh. And Mandy did, too. Horrifying moment when your camera switches direction on its own.

FIRST OF THE CLASS

I was sitting in First Class and I was NOT going to move.

The flight attendant gave me a hard, stern look.

"Not moving," I said quickly.

Why should I move? I was in First Class! *First Class!* I wasn't going anywhere!

I had heard rumors that although my accumulation of frequent flier miles wasn't going to get me to Europe, if I played my cards right, it would land me in a big leather seat in first class for absolutely nothing. It worked like this: if there was a seat that a rich person didn't spend a ridiculous amount on just so that they could get free drinks and eat fancier peanuts, all I had to do was flash my frequent flier card and I was upgraded to sit among the chosen people.

Right.

For almost two years, I had been flashing that card as soon as I checked in, but it was always met with a disdainful look that seemed to say, "You....*silly peasant person!* How dare you think your kind could slip into the elite section! Back to the cattle car with you! Why, you're just lucky we even let you people *sit down!*"

But I wasn't about to give up on my dream. I'll hunt something down for the rest of my life if there's a chance I can get it for free or a relatively good discount. My little corn-teeth have elongated to the length of Julia Robert's horse choppers because I can't seem to find time to floss, but if I can get $3.00 off a bag of kitty litter with the right coupon, I'll pursue it harder than I did a husband.

Then, last week when I was returning from a little vacation in California, a miracle happened. Either the ticket counter girl was new or had just come back from smoking crack in the bathroom, because when I flashed my card and said, "I know I've got a better chance of growing a third breast, but...", she smiled and gave me a ticket that said "First Class" at the bottom.

I couldn't believe it. It was simply unbelievable. Even as I lifted my carry-on into the first class luggage compartment and took my seat, I was convinced I was moments away from being discovered. I was sure the spotlight would be pointed directly on my Jethro rope belt and my status as a commoner with a free upgrade would be revealed.

But amazingly, no one seemed to notice. It was as if just being in First Class gave you a special air, a certain distinction, and before you knew it, you had a fake accent just like Madonna's. I suddenly felt different, although that very well could have been attributed to the fact that I was sucking in my stomach extra hard and I don't think very much oxygen was getting to my brain.

As people—well, who are we kidding?—*coach passengers* were still getting on the plane, the stewardess brought me a Pepsi in a real glass and a guy that looked like a football player took the First Class seat beside me. The stewardess brought him a white wine and after he stretched out to relax, he leaned over and whispered, "Did you hear that? I swear the guy in front of us just said he's in porn!"

I emitted a high-class chortle, as I imagined the way a Vanderbilt would laugh, which sounded like a very drawn-out, "Haaa, haaaa, haaaa..."

"Well, the gentleman also mentioned he was from Sierra Vista," I said as I leaned over and said with a smirk on my face and my teeth clenched. "So I do indeed believe, my dear fellow First Classmate, that his area of financiality is not *porn* but... *corn.* Haaa, haaa, haaa..."

He laughed and suddenly pointed at a coach-class passenger just boarding the plane. "Hey!" he whispered again. "I know that guy! See him, right there? He's the most famous horse trainer in the world! His horses have won the Kentucky Derby and the Triple Crown! He's loaded!"

Oh no, I thought, I wasn't prepared for rich people horse talk! I know nothing about horses except that we had the same teeth due to gum recession!

Suddenly, from across the aisle, a woman turned to us and said, "If he's so loaded, why is he sitting...*back there?*"

"Haaaa, haaaa, haaaa..." we all laughed.

It was then that I noticed an inordinate amount of maintenance people boarding the craft and talking with the pilot, who then whispered to the stewardess who then picked up the intercom microphone. "We're sorry to announce that due to a mechanical failure, this flight has been canceled," she informed us. "We'll do our best to accommodate you on other flights."

Everyone started getting off the plane. But I just wanted to cherish it a little bit longer. I wasn't ready to go back to being a peasant with bleeding gums who used coupons for kitty litter. I had passed for a rich person; didn't that mean anything?

Apparently not, because the same stewardess who gave me the Pepsi in the real, live glass was looking at me and pointing her thumb at the cabin door.

"I'm not moving," I said to her. "I seem to have misplaced my... treasure."

"Move it, Ellie Mae," the stewardess replied. "You can fool all of the other upgrades, but you can't fool me."

"Fine," I said gathering my stuff. "What do think my chances are of getting First Class on the next flight?"

The stewardess looked at me and smiled.

"Haaaa, haaaa, haaaa," she said.

Dear homeless person who turned my wallet in after finding it in the Safeway parking lot: Thank you for being a good citizen and not running off with my credit cards or selling my ID. I don't doubt it was you who left the stink cloud in the wine aisle, and now I forgive you. I hope that the Little Caeser's pizza and Cheesy Sticks you bought with the nine dollars you stole from my wallet was as fresh and hot as they promise. And super thanks for not wiping your ass with it.
Awesomely, Laurie

THE FIXER

Drip, drip, drip.

You could hear it from any room in the house; the sound followed us from room to room like a restless spirit, demanding to be put to rest.

Drip, drip, drip.

"I've got to fix that thing," my husband said every time he passed by the kitchen sink and the faucet that sobbed relentlessly.

Drip, drip, drip.

I, on the other hand, had no choice but to laugh. By the time that faucet got fixed, I was convinced that I would probably be married to somebody else.

In any case, the mere thought of him fixing anything was preposterous, since I will freely admit that I married for love and because it seemed like the next logical step to me after stalking him got a little boring. I did not marry for money, status, or for my own personal Norm Abrahams slave. I knew he wasn't bringing the assets of a manly assortment of Craftsman tools to the marriage; the man could barely work a flashlight, which he would try to shine on me when I hovered outside his bedroom windows at night, though it looked more like a strobe light. Instead, he brought a guitar, the flashlight and the complete works of Shakespeare, all of which is almost not even worth suing over. I married my husband because he is the nicest man in the world, and I am the meanest girl, which I thought might bring me extra bargaining points with God after I died and was negotiating my release from becoming Mrs. Satan.

But my husband, leery after I hired a homeless man to tear down a tree in our front yard with his bare hands and a couple of kicks, tried to take some matters into his own hands. One day, we were out in the front yard trying to fix a fence when he suddenly screwed me. I was holding two planks together when the power screwdriver, naturally controlled by my husband, unexpectedly leapt ten inches as the tip plowed and then drilled into my hand. It ripped into one of the latex gardening gloves I was wearing, tearing it to shreds, which, in turn, began whipping around wildly with the determined vibrations of the screwdriver. My husband, understanding the ripped latex to be small flags of my flesh, began screaming, although he was not horrified enough to remove the screwdriver from my body. With my non-crucified hand, I knocked the screwdriver from his, but at least I got something good out of it. The next time I saw my mom, I was able to hold out my palm and say to her, "Look, Ma. I told you I was good. *Stigmata*."

When it came time to paint the house, he claimed that once he reached the top rung of the ladder, he saw a bright, welcoming light and heard angels call his name. To scare him into climbing back up, I told him if he didn't finish it, I'd pay my ex-boyfriend to paint the house, a threat I was forced to follow up on.

As he was installing a ceiling fan, a micro particle of plaster landed in his eye, and rendered him completely blind until the electrician left with a check in his hand.

But honestly, this isn't all bad. If he *could* fix things, word would get out and I'd have to fend off hordes of women with a Taser. He'd become the catch of the century and I'd be alone with nobody to blame stuff on. And to be truthful, he can fix one thing. When the toilet won't stop running, my husband is an expert at sticking his hand into the slimy tank and putting the rubber stopper back over the hole. I was so thrilled when he learned to do this that at parties, I'd move the stopper with his toothbrush and then call my friends in while he performed the miraculous repair.

When I couldn't take the drip, drip, drip of the kitchen faucet for one second more, I did the only thing I could. I hit it with a rock. A couple of times. Pretty hard. I guess hard enough to break a rather important part of it, because the faucet didn't drip anymore. Instead, it just ran, refusing to shut off.

"I don't know what happened," I explained to my husband when he came home and stood staring at the faucet. "I'm thinking maybe it got struck by lightening, because that would explain all of those dents."

He took a deep breath and left the house, and when he came back, he was carrying a Lowe's bag with all kinds of stuff in it.

"What are you doing?" I asked as he approached the sink with something that looked like a wrench.

"I'm fixing the faucet!" he answered.

"Stay away from me with that thing!" I said. "I'm just starting to get the feeling back in my fingertips!"

He removed the faucet handle.

"Are you hearing voices yet?" I queried.

He took out a teeny part and replaced it with a new one from the bag.

"Don't let any of those washers fall in your eye!" I warned.

He put the faucet handle back, and turned the water on.

And then, we both watched in amazement as he turned the faucet off, and the water stopped. No rush, no drip. He had fixed it.

"Oh, God," I sighed. "You're going to start dating now, aren't you?"

"Are you kidding?" he laughed. "I'm the catch of the century! But I'm going to have to fix that flashlight first."

"For old time's sake," I said wearily, "Do me a favor and fix the toilet before you go. It got hit by a rock."

So last night when I was reading in bed, by husband pointed to the back book cover and said, "What's that on your book? Is that...ham?"
I took a look and said, "Well, I just had a ham snack before I came to bed. I guess some stuck."
He looked at me for a moment and said, "You are a sad lady."

FIRECRACKERS MY ASS

BAM!

"Not again," my husband said, turning over and hitting his pillow. "I can't take much more of this."

In the darkness of our unlit bedroom on the Fourth of July last year, I could feel his frustration, but mainly because felt it myself.

Pop! Pop! Pop! Pop! Pop!

"This is ridiculous!" I pouted, sitting up to see the red glow of the clock. "It's 4:16 in the morning! Why are they still setting off firecrackers?"

"Those aren't firecrackers," my husband said, muffled underneath the pillow he had now placed over his head. "Those are gunshots. People are shooting off guns!"

Our neighbors, inebriated beyond the point that they could vocalize their own legal names, were pointing firearms at the sky and pulling the trigger. And it wasn't just one neighbor, either; from the sounds of it, there was apparently a sky shooter on each block, so full of joy and patriotism that they celebrated the right to bear arms by staggering onto their roofs or rotting backyard picnic tables and assuming the bad personality traits of Patty Hearst.

Newscasters warn folks about the dangers of gun play every Fourth of July. Newspapers run front-page stories. And every fifth of July, we're informed about children that were hit by a stray bullet from their uncle's gun that either left them paralyzed or dead. Most parties I've gone to typically don't end with a family huddling together in a hospital waiting room. I once saw a friend snap her ankle in half, however, but that just because she was River Dancing with a quart of tequila in her. As she fell to the ground, her inebriation resulted in a second tragedy that night as her lit cigarette catapulted across the patio, landed on my Kate Spade purse and caught it on fire.

It didn't cross anyone's mind to try to top that kind of fun by flashing a .45. What's the rule at these shooting gatherings—It's not a party until someone needs a transfusion?

I'd call it a DUI all right—Dorks Under the Influence. Not that drunk people ordinarily perform acts of genius, but this defies the even the basic laws of common sense. Do the party guests packing heat think that bullets are gravity-defying, or that if lead travels high enough will get sucked into a planetary orbit and become space junk?

I'm not going to place this blame solely on men with guns, either. I know there have got to be some women out there that partake, but I also want to know where the wives, girlfriends and mothers of these shooters are then they're sending rounds airborne in the middle of the night. They can't be sleeping. I'm not. I'm not suggesting they wrestle away a gun from their drunk counterpart, I'm suggesting that either 1) at the point that excessive inebriation becomes obvious (i.e.: the shooter vomits on a pet, walks around with his fly unzipped and his belt undone or heads to Taco Bell for a midnight snack, HIDE THE GUNS. 2) Or there's an even simpler solution. Mention, gently and yet firmly "Honey, this is not a good idea. You could kill one of our kids."

Personally, the only experience I've ever had with bullets involved my dog, Max, who dragged a box of them that belonged to a roommate into the backyard and dumped it into the grass. The seven people I lived with and I scoured the grass on our hands and knees for hours, but only came up with 34 bullets, 16 shy of what was needed to fill a complete box, because Max had eaten the rest. He turned out to be fine, although we were unable to mow the grass in the backyard because we were afraid that the lawnmower blades would dig up a bullet we had missed and would inevitably fly around the yard until it lodged in someone's neck.

My friend Jim and I worked up a solution to this problem, but it's a community effort. We figure if we can manufacture a spot that will attract jackasses on holidays, we could secure them all in one spot outside of the city limits, like at Compton Terrace or the driving track. We could build a little village, stocked with concession booths selling corndogs and any kind of meat skewered on a stick. We'd bring the cheap beer in, and set up tents with topless dancers and wait for sundown.

We want to name this spot "Guntown." It would render the rest of the community safe, and we wouldn't need to advertise or anything. We just need to create the proper environment, set up a couple of single-wide trailers and lots of cars without wheels, and believe me, the masses will come. Now, Guntown is not for NRA members, hunters or people that employ licensed weapons for security purposes. The only people allowed in Guntown are those with high tendencies to load up on the hooch and start shooting with absolutely no provocation whatsoever.

What's even better is that this could be used as a deterrent to sky shooting, much like the death sentence is to murder. Anyone charged with illegally shooting off a firearm would get sent to Guntown, but SOBER. Just to make them understand how horrifying a drunk, round-bellied man with a piece of chewed hot dog on his lip is when he's got a loaded weapon secured in his wobbling hand.

Think that's scary?

Come to my house on the Fourth. We can have a barbecue, eat some pie, and when the sun starts to set, we'll all huddle in the hallway and wait for my neighbors to begin the war.

GERMOGRAPHY

"What," my husband said slowly, "have you done now?"

"It's a protective layer over the bed," I said excitedly as I beamed, looking up at the canopy I had installed from the ceiling that draped over our bed. "It's going to protect us from germs as we sleep!"

My husband reached out and touched the canopy with his hand.

"I'm not sleeping under that," he replied in a low voice as he just stared at my creation.

"Think of how SAFE you'll feel," I added, trying to convince him.

"SAFE?" he nearly yelled as he turned toward me. "SAFE? You used plastic drop cloths! You've made a bed in a plastic bubble! That's not safe! It's a queen-sized body bag!"

My husband didn't know what he was talking about. He hadn't seen what I saw earlier in the day, which was a Discovery Health Channel show about how people get sick.

There, on the TV, was Holly, a girl who was standing in an elevator with a man who was getting ready to destroy her life.

He coughed on her.

Poor Holly. There she was, completely unaware while millions of minute mucous particles, each carrying the flu virus, exploded into the air like rain. It was their germ mission to land on her and try to find their way into an opening of her body, much like date I once had. Then, one successful particle invaded her through her nose. It was all over.

I knew how Holly felt, because I've been sick three times since fall, and I wasn't about to let it happen again. In fact, I suspected that my most recent illness was due a lady at work who got into an elevator I was in, and coughed all over me like she was an agent of the Taliban before she got off on the next floor. Now that I had seen Holly's show and knew how germs worked, I was going to protect myself. And putting up a protective barrier around my bed was the first step.

My husband, however, saw danger.

"Take that down," he insisted. "I can see just it now. I'm going to get all tangled up in it and suffocate like a dolphin in a net!"

"You don't understand," I said emphatically. "There are germs everywhere, just waiting to set up shop in your mucous membranes! We have to be careful! I'm a germophobe now!"

"A germophobe, huh?" my husband replied. "Well, you're not a very good one. You're sick more than a toddler in daycare. Is this another ploy to qualify for disability, because I'm telling you, you are one manic cycle away from getting your own caseworker! I mean, I thought you were odd when we were dating, but I always attributed it to the alcohol!"

"I'm trying to save us BOTH," I asserted.

"Why can't you have another hobby?" my husband pleaded, "Like exercise or dusting? Laundry would be a *very* good hobby for you. Think of how healthy we could be if we actually had clean clothes!"

I just ignored him. I was concentrating on germs. From now on, I decided, shaking hands with people was out of the question. Instead, I would just say, "Nice to meet you," and then wave at them energetically or blow them a kiss. There was no way I would touch a public door knob, since Holly's show had shown me it was the equivalent of sticking your hand into the toilet in a Port-O-Potty. The surface of a door knob holds a lottery of sickness, not to mention bits from people's bodies. I used a paper towel shield or pushed the door open with my rear end, since that area is usually protected by a very firm and impenetrable butt shaper, and germs seeking refuge down there would simply bounce off of the industrial-quality lycra.

Touch a hand rail on an escalator? You've got to be kidding! Those things are nothing more than a conveyor belt of pestilence and filth, serving up a buffet of maladies and horror that would rival any petri dish in the labs at the Center for Disease Control. Grab onto one of those things and you're toying with unleashing the Apocalypse. Then we have shopping carts equipped with handles acting as a flu and cold lightening rod, and don't forget about airplanes that recirculate air, creating a fan that spews out a hotbed of various afflictions. And I ever heard someone cough, I'd sprint the other way like an Olympic athlete on some very good drugs.

As it turned out, people were coughing everywhere I went, too, and in one day alone, I ran farther than my frequent flier miles would get me. People were sick everywhere. Germs were everywhere, and running away all of the time was making me very tired. The only truly safe place where I could go and not push myself to the point of exhaustion, I figured, was my house. So I just stayed inside, protected from the seething world of germs, watching TV.

The next day when my husband came home, he headed straight for the bedroom with a pair of scissors in his hands.

"That's it!" he shouted as he walked down the hallway. "I've had it! I spent the whole night breathing through a straw poked through the body bag! I'm not doing it again!"

"You're right," I said as I watched him cut it down. "You're totally right. I'm not a germophobe anymore. It's way too much work. But today, I watched this show on Discovery Health, and did you know that parasites and tapeworms that can grow as long as 11 feet can get into your body through food and water if you don't take the proper precautions? Did you? DID YOU?"

So I just went and filled up my gas tank, and the attendant was so nice she tried to scrub the moss off of my back window. So I gave her a dollar tip. She smiled and said "Thank you!" so I gave her something even more valuable. "I just saw your co-worker pick his nose," I whispered, "and then roll it up with his fingers like a little ball. Don't touch anything he's touched!"

So yesterday at Powell's bookstore in Portland, we actually got to park in the garage, which is a miracle. But we had to climb down more stairs than a lighthouse to get to the bottom. When we were leaving, I asked the booth attendant if there was an elevator.

"Who need elevator?" he asked.

"I don't need it, but I'd like it," I replied.

"Why you need elevator?" he asked.

"I have no cartilage in my right knee," I said, which he understood as "I am a fat lady that does not like to move."

"No," he replied disgustedly. "No elevator. You stay here. He come pick you up."

I took the stairs because I didn't want to be stuck at the bottom next to the booth guy, who I was sure was about to start yelling at passersby, "Chubby want elevator! Maybe she take stairs, she not so round!", but regretted it the moment I did, and as I met my husband, who had been waiting for me at the top for ten minutes, he said, "Um, I've never seen anyone stair shamed before."

GOOD WILL TO ALL AND TO ALL A GOOD WILL

I thought I was so smart.

I really thought that calling the charity donation line and arranging for a pick-up was the best thing I could have done to make myself get rid of all of the old stuff laying around the house so we could make room for all of the new stuff we got over the holidays. This way, I'd be forced to have something waiting on the front porch when the donation truck arrived.

I was so smart.

"Okay," I announced to my husband the day before the pick-up date. "Go get all of your junk. We're giving it away tomorrow to the less fortunate."

"Junk?" my husband questioned. "I don't have any junk. In case you don't remember, I'm *married*, which means the only junk I'm allowed to have has to be pre-approved by my wife before I bring it in the house, at which point it therefore loses it's 'junk' status and moves to the 'treasured belongings' category."

"You must think that you're talking to the wife who doesn't know that you often bring junk into this house while she's pretend sleeping and too tired to get up to do an inspection," I snipped. "Now go into that closet of yours and bring out that floor-length black fake leather coat your brother gave you. If you were spotted wearing it behind the wheel of a Lincoln Continental, I'd have to explain to a lot of people why I married a pimp."

"But I was saving it for a Halloween costume and it makes my shoulders look broad in relation to my waist!" my husband whined. "Frankly, I don't understand why the less fortunate are allowed to have junk and I'm not. That doesn't sound less fortunate to me, that sounds like FREEDOM."

"Freedom's just another word for nothing left to lose, Huggy Bear," I answered. "And you are closer to it than you think! Now go rustle up that coat and that stinky pair of Birkenstocks you pretend to not have."

"That is not fair," he protested. "What are *you* going to donate to the less fortunate? What about that broken-down fan that's so loud when it's on that we didn't hear the band of thieves that stole the patio set which was right outside our bedroom window?"

"Oh, you are insane!" I argued back. "That fan is still good; it still has one blade! And I need the white noise it makes so I can sleep!"

"That's not white noise! That's all the parts inside the motor crashing together! You know, you have so much junk in this house that I can close my eyes and randomly touch a junk object," my husband said as he closed his eyes, reached his arms out and snatched something off the coffee table. "Look! Junk! Here's something you can give away, or do you have a good reason why you need to hang onto this Homer Simpson Pez?"

"See? That's how much *you* know," I replied. "That Homer Simspon Pez has a better investment return than a 401K! Do you know that in 10 years, I can probably sell it on eBay for *ten dollars* when it only cost me 49 cents? Do you? That 'junk' just happens to be your future, buddy!"

"Is my future wearing a Norma Kamali tube dress that would barely fit over a Barbie?" he asked. "Because there's one draped over the broken fan in the bedroom right now that I've only seen you wear in photos, and the guy next to you was wearing parachute pants and eyeliner!"

"I *will* fit into that dress again when it eventually comes back into style!" I insisted. "I just need an incentive to break my addiction to processed sugar, like a diabetes diagnosis!"

"Focus?" my husband questioned. "You'd need to fall into a coma and have your feeding tube come loose! I have socks that are bigger than that dress! I don't even think the cat could wear it without getting arrested!"

"Well, you should know, pimp!" I pouted. "Hands off my junk!"

"Oh yeah?" he countered. "Then hands off *my* junk!"

"Fine!" I yelled.

"Fine!" my husband yelled back.

But the next morning, when the donation truck pulled up and two men got out, they walked to the front porch, took a good look at the one bladed fan, the fake leather pimp coat and the Norma Kamali tube sock, and I swear I heard one of them say to the other, "Jeez. Now this is junk!"

Dear Mom:

I know the norovirus is very dangerous because 80-year olds die on cruise ships all the time from it, but the reason I didn't go to Urgent Care was because:

1) Urgent Care is the payday loan of medical providers;

2) The smell of the Dominos next door on one side and the Jimmy John's on the other would have made me hurl;

3) Who ever is sitting in the waiting room has something far worse and more contagious than I do;

4) the last time I went, the "Dr." was a dead ringer for the person outside holding a "Hungry and Pregnant" sign and had just come back from a cigarette break. I think I would rather go to a witch doctor, because witch doctors never graduate last in their class and at least I wouldn't be kidding myself. Pull a chicken liver out of my neck and call it a day.

THE HAGGLER

Jamie wanted to haggle.

"I just want to haggle once," she said as she and I strolled the aisles of the Pasadena Flea Market. "I've got Bargain Fever! I'm starving for a bargain!"

We were certainly in the right place. The flea market stretched far beyond what our human eyes could see, full of vendors that wanted the cold-hard cash that we had stuffed in our wallets.

Being that I had once read an article about haggling in a women's magazine in my mom's bathroom, I became the self-appointed leader of our bargain expedition.

"We need to bring cash," I told her the night before during the Pre-Pasadena Flea Market Meeting in her living room. "Dealers will give you *big* discounts if you have cash."

She nodded.

"And it's important that you turn the odds in your favor," I continued. "Like mentioning that the dealer is wearing a flattering, slimming color, asking them what kind of perfume they're wearing or if they're free for a drink later. Break down the barrier, show them that you're a friend, and grease them up like a pig."

"I don't like the drink part," Jamie said. "That sounds like something I might get arrested for."

I sighed. "How bad do you want a bargain? Because you know, I can't work with you if you won't work with me," I said harshly. "I'm the expert! I'm the one who read the article! OKAY?"

My pupil nodded again.

"OKAY!" I said excitedly. "Now we need to get an early start, because it starts at seven a.m. I'm thinking we should get there a little before the crowd of shopping maggots descend. Sloppy seconds are no fun! I think we should leave now."

"That would be a good idea," Jamie agreed. "Since you don't have a car here and I do, and I'm planning on getting there at 6:59 a.m., it will take you about 12 hours to walk to Pasadena! Unless, that is, you read an article in your mom's bathroom about hitch hiking."

At 6:59 the next morning, we entered the flea market.

"Now don't buy the first thing you see," I advised Jamie. "Take your time, look around, don't be hasty. Ooooh, what's that?!"

I shot over to a nearby table as she followed.

"How much for this vase?" I asked the dealer as I picked it up.

"Forty-five," the dealer replied, barely looking at me.

"I have cash," I countered, bringing out my wallet.

The dealer paused for a moment, and I could feel his guard drop as his belly peeked out from above his waist band.

"Forty-four," he finally said.

"That Bob Seger concert T-shirt makes you look so thin," I said, greasing up the pig.

"It's not the shirt," he retorted. "It's the cancer in my gut eating me from the inside out."

"Sold for forty-five!" I said, handing over a part of my money roll.

"Boy, you're as smooth as your complexion," Jamie said.

"The article didn't say anything about haggling with the terminally ill," I snapped back.

We rounded the first corner and a latter across the aisle caught my eye. I grabbed for it and turned it over to see the markings.

I gasped. "V-N-I-H-O! I can't believe it!" I whispered to Jamie. "V. Niho was a porcelain artisan of the 1700's! I just saw this same thing on Antiques Roadshow and one of those creepy twins said it would sell at auction for $6,000!"

I put the platter back down and tried to act nonchalant. "How much are you looking to get for the platter?" I asked to the woman behind the table.

"I'd take 50," she said.

"Now that's what I call a bargain!" I nearly yelled and peeled a couple more layers from my money roll.

As we walked on to the next aisle, Jamie casually asked if she could see the V. Niho platter.

"Okay," I said reluctantly, handing it over. "But be careful, *please*! A porcelain god made that! That plate's going to pay for my Chinese baby!"

Jamie turned it over and studied the marking. "V-N-I-H-O, huh?" she said. "Chinese baby, huh? That's so funny. Because if you turn this platter upside down, it looks like the letters C-H-I-N-A but a little smeared. Maybe V. Niho—the porcelain god—is sending you a sign. Because I think you bought a turd."

And then she laughed so hard she got a cramp.

When she looked up, her laughter ceased, and she gravitated toward a booth like a hungry mosquito to a fat man's thigh.

She didn't say anything as she extended her hands and picked up an antique, framed map of the whole world.

"I want it," she said almost in a coo, and then showed me the panic in her eyes. "I want to haggle, but I don't think I can do it! Can you.... help me? Will you help me?"

I looked at the $80 price tag, then to the relatively healthy appearing dealer. "Piece of cake," I whispered back.

The dealer strutted over and stood before us. "You like that?" he questioned with a smile.

I opened my mouth to make him an offer.

"NOT FOR EIGHTY BUCKS I DON'T!!!!" Jamie roared.

"SIXTY!" he yelled back.

"FORTY!" she bid.

"DEAL!" he said.

We stood there for a moment in silence as the dealer wrapped up the map.

"I'm going to get a lemonade icee," I said solemnly.

"Get me one, too," Jamie said. "Being a Bargain Queen is thirsty work."

I sauntered up to the cart with cash in my hand, and put on my meanest haggling face. I wasn't going to leave the flea market without getting at least one deal, since the sign said $2.42 and I only had $3 left.

"Let's make a deal," I said to the vendor, holding out the stiff, hard cash. "I'll give you three bucks for two icees."

"Oooh, a haggler, huh?" he said with a sly grin.

"You got that right," I said, happy that I was finally identified.

"You've got yourself a deal," he said, handing over the two icees and plucking the $3 from my hand.

With her map, Jamie came over and took her icee.

"I got both of these for THREE BUCKS!" I giggled excitedly.

"Wow, you've outdone yourself today," she said, looking at the icee sign. "Especially since it says two icees for two dollars!"

I was forced to get a new computer. I was married to my old one for eight years. We had seven books together. I set up the new one last night. It's like dating someone half my age. It has all these moves I don't understand. It speaks in a language that I only half get. It moves way too fast and thinks everything is about IT. And then, when I walked out of the room last night, I swear I heard it laughing at me.

AND NO ONE SAID ANYTHING

"Nope!" I yelled as I ran my fingers through my hair. "Shorter!"

"Are you sure?" my friend Kryssi said, her scissors pulled back as she stood there, hesitantly. "It's already pretty short."

"SHORTER!" I commanded. "I can't stand long hair for one more minute!"

I had grown tired of my coif, the Ted Kaczynski-like bush that grew on my head. It was unruly, wiry and I've seen better hairdos on homeless people. One day last week, I looked in the mirror and realized what I saw: I looked like an old hippie woman that grew mushrooms in her bathtub and then sold them to kids at Phish concerts. Something had to be done.

It had to go. Admittedly, I was taking a risk, since I had been told before by a hair dresser that cutting my hair above my ears would draw attention to my flapping jowls and turkey neck, but I brushed those warnings aside as I yelled to Kryssi to cut me again. I knew what I wanted; my destiny hair taunted me for thirteen weeks in a row as Colleen repeatedly popped up on *Survivor*, her jungle island hair tousled perfectly, a delectable sexy mess. I knew that as soon as I had that haircut, I would also assume her celestial beauty and bewitching charisma. At my urging, Kryssi went back in for the kill, although I swear I heard her mumble that the job would be far easier had she had a weed eater at her disposal.

After she lopped off the last couple of inches, she brushed me off and pointed me toward the mirror.

I took a gander.

Looking back at me was not Colleen, I saw no jungle kitten, no tropical, sun-kissed Lolita.

I saw Janet Napolitano.

"You said 'shorter'!" Kryssi said as she ran to get me a tissue to clean up my burst of emotion. "That's what you said!"

"I said I wanted to look like Colleen," I stressed.

"But Colleen is pretty," Kryssi said, trying to console me with a hug. "And I'm charging you for that broken mirror."

I rushed home, still wrapped in the newborn stages of optimism, positive that with a little gel and a couple of big infected wounds on my legs, people would be flocking to me for Colleen's autograph.

Unfortunately, my husband's car was parked in the driveway when I got there, so covering my head with both arms, I rushed into the house and started for the bathroom.

"Let's see!" he said as he struggled to pull my arms away, despite my protests. After a brief battle that landed me on the floor, silence enveloped the room as my head was exposed.

"Where did you go?" he said quietly. "To Kryssi's or did you stop by the recruitment office to enlist?"

"That's not fair!" I retorted, scrambling up. "All I need is some styling products to make me into Colleen!"

"But Colleen is pretty," he emphasized. "She's a tantalizing jungle kitten with a fiery, carnal spirit, begging to be tamed."

"And me?" I asked.

"Well, if I were you, I'd play it safe and stay indoors come November. With that neck exposed, you could find yourself shot, plucked and filled with Stove Top stuffing on someone's dining room table," he answered. "Believe me, that's not an attractive position for you."

I gasped. "The policy is that 'things in the bedroom stay in the bedroom!'" I yelled as I slammed the bathroom door.

I got out my gel and went to work. I styled. I blow tried. I curled. I put a little barrette in front. When I was done, I realized I was now Ethel Mertz.

I got a sinking, black feeling that swallowed my stomach. What had I done? Kryssi was right, I had gone too short. This would take months to grow out. My hair was a disaster. There was no way around it, unless I started telling people that I was enrolled in a new medical test that combined chemotherapy, radiation and electrolysis. I thought about calling Kryssi to ask her if she still had some of my hair, and if she thought we could glue it back, but she said she already sold it to someone who makes clown wigs.

When I went to work the next day, I didn't feel any better, especially when I received the worst kind of response from my co-workers: Nothing. Okay, I got some double-takes, but other than that, everyone tried to ignore it like a whitehead on the side of my nose.

My family wasn't that reserved. When I walked into my mom's house, my dad saluted me and my mother shook her head.

"I knew it! I knew it!" she said as she stared at me. "This is it. This is when she tells us she likes girls!"

"Not all girls," I said, hanging my head. "Just Colleen."

"Colleen, the exquisite seductress from the island?" my dad said. "But she's pretty! That playful, wind-whipped hair, tossed with sensuality and splendor."

"Maybe I should go shorter," my mother said, touching the base of her neck.

LIGHTS OUT

The moment I heard the crack of the tree breaking in half in my front yard was the same moment the lights went dead inside my house. The wind of the monsoon storm outside whistled viciously as I waited for the lights to come back on.

After several minutes in the dark, my husband found the flashlight.

"They'll come back on in a minute," he assured me. "The neighbor's lights are still on."

"What if they don't come back on?" I replied. "It's starting to get hot in here."

"You know, this is just like on the prairie," my husband said quickly and wisely. "This is like living as pioneers! Laura Ingalls Wilder had to live just like this!"

"Oh my God! You're right!" I said excitedly. "We're like prairie people! You light the oil lamp and I'll get my sunbonnet!"

"Go get the fiddle, Ma!" he joked as he took the glass globe off the lamp and lit the wick.

"Oh my God!" I said suddenly. "You know what else?"

"We're not going to milk the dog, are we?" he asked cautiously.

I just looked at him through the shadows. "I don't know what weird pioneer fantasies you get in your head when the lights go out," I said harshly, "But I was just going to suggest that we can break out the camp stove, the gallon can of pork 'n beans and the chemical toilet we had left over from our Year 2000 survival kit!"

"You sure can spell P-A-R-T-Y! But I don't think we should be using propane indoors because I really enjoy having skin on my body," my husband said. "Besides, cooking might make it hotter in here."

I nodded as the first bead of sweat ran down the side of my face. "Maybe we should call the power company and see when the power is going to come back on," I added.

My husband took the flashlight and went to find the phone. When the rain stopped, it instantly started to get even hotter. The air was still, stifled, almost dead. It was if someone draped a massive heating blanket over our whole house and wanted to suffocate us.

"They said the power will be back on by 1:30," he said, coming back into the room.

"But it's 11:30 now," I answered. "That's two hours! What did you tell them?"

"I said, 'Hey, we really need our power! We have pets!'" he answered. "But they didn't seem too impressed."

"It is so hot in here," I moaned in the dark.

"Hey," my husband said. "You know what they say about blackouts."

"What?" I replied. "That they kill the old and weak?"

"No. After blackouts like this, a bunch of babies are always born nine months later," he suggested.

I paused for a moment. "I don't know if you can see my face," I said as two more beads of sweat rolled down my forehead, one balanced on my nose and a whole convoy trekked down the valley of my butt, "But the look on it says 'Closed for Business Until Further Notice. Off Limits Unless Patron Can Find A Generator. Guard Dog Will Bite His Sweaty Little Face Off.' If I feel anything except ice touching me in the dark, I will cut you, boy."

"You know, people pay lots of money for this kind of heat," my husband said, trying to be positive. "People go to spas to sit in saunas for hundreds of dollars. Think of all the money we're saving."

"Well, with the money we save, we can buy a pair of real nice coffins," I said snidely. "Maybe the power company can say the eulogy: 'They were Equalizer Customers, and they almost paid their bills on time. Unfortunately, that wasn't enough for us to want to save their lives.'"

It was getting hotter.

"Tomorrow, we should move to Oregon," I suggested as perspiration began to soak my scalp. "Because this is inhumane. *I am suffering.* I could steam rice in my bra. You know, this is when it totally pays off to buy the house next door to the governor's. I bet she's sleeping under a working fan right now."

"Oh, jeez," my husband said suddenly, looking at his chest. "I just felt my right lung just liquefy."

"It's like an oven in here," I said, fanning myself with our last electric bill. "We're being cooked. Oh, God. I'm a Boston Chicken! *I'm a Boston Chicken!*"

"Please don't freak out, honey," my husband said, trying to calm me. "With the streetlight across the street reflecting off all of the sweat on your body, you look like the Milky Way."

"The electricity isn't going to come back on at 1:30, is it?" I asked fearfully.

"Unless the Easter Bunny, Tooth Fairy and Rudolph the Red-Nosed Reindeer are real," my husband said matter-of-factly. "No, Virginia, the power company will not fix the power by 1:30. It's just a fable. I'm sorry."

"OK," I said calmly and laid myself back down, not knowing whether the stuff streaming down my face was sweat or tears.

I had a dream last night that I was a backup singer for Creedence Clearwater Revival. The thing I remember most clearly is the lead singer telling me, "It is okay that you don't know the words, but you have to stop falling off of the stage."

HEATWAVE HOTEL

"So you have a room available?" I asked the fellow on the other end of the line. "A room for this evening?"

"Oh, yes," he confirmed. "I have 48 rooms and it is summer in Phoenix. Which means I have 48 empty rooms."

"Now you have 47," I added. "And... will you take pets?"

"Well," the fellow said, pausing. "We're really not supposed to, but as long as it's a small dog or a cat, I guess that would be okay."

"Oh, yes. Yes, they're small dogs," I said, wondering how I was going to pass off a Labrador and a German Shepard as Pekinese show pooches. I would figure that out later, I thought to myself, right now it didn't matter. All that mattered was getting out of that house.

The night before, a monsoon storm had knocked the crap out of our power supply at 11:30. The hours that followed had been horrible. After filling our hearts with empty promises that our power would be back on two hours after the outage, the power company had not come through. At 2 a.m., the oil lamp flickered its last lick of light, and the house went completely dark.

It felt like a tomb. The hot, still air filled the house like death, with the only sounds the hot, steaming panting of my dogs and the sweat dripping from my body onto the floor breaking the quiet.

At first light, my husband and I threw on clean clothes, filled three pots up with water for the dogs and we left for work.

When I came home that night, I pulled into the driveway hopeful that a cool blast of wind would greet me as soon as I opened the door. As I turned the key in the lock, however, something different hit me altogether.

You have no idea how hot 109 degrees is until you can't get away from it. Until it's in your house, spreading it's evil around like a big, hot virus. Pure unadulterated, undiluted hot STINK. Stink from the heated trash can in the kitchen, stink from the now-spoiled food in the refrigerator, and stink from the general aroma of our house that we otherwise keep covered up with Glade and aromatherapy candles.

I plugged my nose and fumbled around for the phone and called the power company, whose customer service representatives (who, in the outside world would actually be considered nothing more than guerilla terrorists wearing headsets) told me quite bluntly, "Yes, I know it's 109 degrees today, but right now, there's 3,000 people in this city without power, and you, simply, are not our priority."

"Oh, yeah?" I retorted as a coat of thick sweat appeared on me from head to toe. "Well as soon as you get deregulated, the whole bunch of you are totally going to hell!"

Then I hung up, called the hotel and made the reservation.

I was ready by the door with a suitcase when my husband came into the house.

"We've got to go!" I screamed as I ran for the car. "Grab a dog! Hurry! Hurry! Get in the car!"

"What about—" my husband started.

"Leave it!" I cried. "Leave it all! There's evil in that house! We've got to go now, while we still can! We may not make it through another night! Don't you feel it? Don't you feel that heat?"

"Oh my God, it's still off," he said suddenly as he picked up the Labrador, who at 14, is the size and weight of a walrus, and ran to the car.

The wheels of my car squealed away as our black little house looked on.

As soon as I walked into the lobby of the hotel, the manager knew who I was.

"I have your room ready," he said with a yellow smile. "It's right off the street so you can take your little dogs out. Did you want smoking?"

"No, we quit," I said, signing the check-in slip.

"Well I've thought about that," the manager said. "But after you've had a sniper trying to pick off your head in a rice paddy, quitting doesn't seem that important. Here's your key."

I found the room, went back to the car and then pulled up behind the back door to smuggle the dogs in quietly. Thanks to their heat exhaustion, even Bella, the dog we believe is possessed by demons, didn't put up a fuss.

Three people walk into the computer repair store three seconds apart. The first one walks up to the counter and begins, "It was a sunny day," and fifteen minutes later concludes with, "and that's when water from the gutter dripped on my laptop. And my whole business is on there. I'm ruined without it." The second person walks up to the counter and pulls out a laptop that is about a foot thick and wants it fixed, even though It basically has a green screen. The third person puts her iMac on the table in the waiting area and begins sighing loudly at the twenty-minute mark and the second man says to her, "who knew this would take so long," but she stares expressionless at him because she hates him and his 50-pound laptop. When the first woman finally leaves and the third person gets up to the counter, she says "It was a sunny day," the girl helping her stares blankly in response because she is s tiny little Asian version of Christian Bale in The Big Short. And an awesome joke dies a painful, wasteful death.

HOLIDAY PARTY RULES

I was walking by the TV last week when an episode of Sonoran Living about how to throw a festive holiday party caught my eye. The featured guests, two police officers, were explaining how several factors were essential to make your party a successful one, and that's when I eagerly pulled up a chair to watch uninterrupted.

Oh, good, I thought, they're going to fork over the recipe for "Johnny Law's Jungle Juice" and I got ready to write it all down, and this is what they said:

"Holiday Prevention Information for those of you who are HOSTING Parties:

'Serve high-protein food, and offer non-alcohol beverages.

'Encourage guests to designate a driver or offer alternative transportation.

'Never serve alcohol to those under the age of 21.

'Don't let guests mix their own drinks and "close the bar" 90 minutes before the party ends.

'Report suspected drunk drivers IMMEDIATELY to area police."

Now, I don't know how many parties those cops have been to in their lives, but in my book, those aren't tips on how to have a successful party; that's a step-by-step list of "How to Completely Alienate Yourself From Anyone You've Ever Known And Make People Enthusiastically Hate You At The Same Time."

OK, now the "serve high protein food" part I can totally agree with, because if you ever lose me at a party, find the cheese platter. Sure, some people call it filler, but I call it "Little Squares of Love," and as far as I'm concerned, there's no reason to answer the door if you don't have little orange cubes with frilly toothpicks stuck in them behind it.

The alternative transportation part--sure, fine, fine, whatever. You want alternative transportation, hire a limo, but all you're getting from me is the recitation of "2525252 Yellow Cab" and my phone in your hand. I mean, I'm throwing a *party* here, I'm not running FedEx. If you positively, absolutely, have to be back home overnight, dude, make some Mormon friends, but don't count on me to be your ride.

Then there's the "never serve alcohol to those under 21" clause, which I guess I can agree with because I'm married, but if I was still dating, I mean, that's like throwing away half of the sea full of very strapping, fetching fish. Perfectly good talent going right to waste. But hey, you know, I want to throw a successful, Holiday prevention Information party, and that means no drunk, sexy, virile youngins', apparently.

And then we have "Don't let guests mix their own drinks and 'close the bar' 90 minutes before the party ends" rule.

Honestly, I'm not even sure what thing I should say first about this.

Um, you know, the last time I had a party that ended at a specific time, I got hit after my friends went home because Rhonda Legarski attached the tape on the tail of the donkey to my mother's brand new red velvet flocked wallpaper.

Ninety minutes before the party ends? How are you supposed to know when THAT is? I mean, when the host flies out a window or is seen passed out in a bathtub or is escorted away in handcuffs THEN I guess you can say, "Wow, we were supposed to stop drinking like 90 minutes ago," but come ON, man! Do you see me with my own TV show talking to dead people? I'm no psychic! I didn't go to school for that! How do I know when the party is going to end? That's a lot of pressure for a party goer, you know! Most of the time I'm not even sure if it's still p.m., let alone try to figure out when every alcoholic at the party is going to burst into a pumpkin!

Oh, and my FAVORITE had to be "report suspected drunk drivers IMMEDIATELY to area police." Oh, sure, yeah. Especially if you want to have another party *next* year. Talk about having five pounds of cheese cubes on your hands. Oh, absolutely, everyone is going to go to your house for a party, especially when you got seven people arrested last year *in your driveway*. "Let's go to Neil's party this year, I think it will be a whole lot more fun than turning myself in," or "You know, Sharon's party is the place to be if you ever wondered what a Field Sobriety Test was like." Sure, it's a good idea, but only if you're running for office.

So beware, folks, if you're invited anywhere this season, you might want to ask if you can peek at the "Party Manifesto" before you commit to an evening of fun that rivals a holding pen at the county jail.

Well, at least there you could say, "You know, you should have stopped drinking 90 minutes ago."

I'M NOT A HELPER

I was just getting all settled in for a nice, comfortable flight back to Phoenix in first class compliments of my frequent flier miles. I had my book, I had my pillow and I was about to take a sip of my pre-flight drink when the flight attendant leaned over and said, "Since you're sitting in the first row, I have to ask you if you would assist me should I need some help. If not, I'll have to move you to another seat."

Frankly, I didn't know what to say, but I did know one thing: I wasn't going BACK THERE. You know what I mean. BACK THERE, the poor part of the plane. If you've never flown UP HERE, my advice is DON'T. Simply don't. Because all it takes is one time to get addicted to UP HERE, and once you've had it, there's no going back. It's like smoking heroin or picking up a dozen at Krispy Kreme. You could smoke all the crack my neighbor makes in his kitchen in one night and not get as high. Compared to first class, everything else is just a rickshaw.

To tell you the truth, I was both caught off guard and determined to stay in my First Class seat, so I hesitantly nodded at the flight attendant.

"Good!" she smiled and said.

And all of a sudden, I knew I had made a big mistake, a tremendous mistake, because I had just made a bigger commitment than I did when I got married. I mean, I agreed to help. *To help!* I'm not a helper. I'm an antagonist. I mean, "help" is a pretty general term, don't you think, it could mean a lot of things. I could mean passing out peanuts, or it could mean wrestling a passenger who's waving around machine gun to the floor. The flight attendants wouldn't want to do that. I mean, of course they'd send out the new helper girl. "No one's attached to her yet and she weighs as much as all four of us!" That's what they'd say. So there I am, the helper, leaping on the back of a terrorist like a feral cat while the flight attendants hide, all four of them together in the soda can cart. I could be taken hostage. That happens to helpers, you know. They're helping, and all of a sudden, they're hog tied and eating bugs in some jungle hut. Of course, I'd probably lose some weight, but then I'd gain it all back anyway when I got over the Post Traumatic Stress "See, That's What You Get For Helping" Syndrome. Or I might achieve my ideal weight from starvation just to end up beheaded as an example to the other hostages. Sure, I'd be able to fit into size 10 DKNY pants I bought on sale two years ago to entice me to lose weight, but how exactly is that positive if I am missing a head? Tabloids would call me the "Headless Hamburger Helper Girl."

Terrific, I thought, just terrific. I am the helper. Now I have to stay alert, I have to be aware of any "help" situations that may arise. I have a bad back, and you know, I didn't go to college to *help*. I can't even read my book now, because every time we hit a bump or hear a noise I'll have to stop, mark my place and think, "Is it Help Time? Is it NOW? Is this my moment of Help?" And I'll tell you right now, I'm not going out onto that wing to fix an engine or something. Not even if they tie a rope around me or promise me extra snacks. No way. You know, I'm no dummy, I know I'm the patsy here. In Lifetime movies, it's always the helper that gets sucked out of the plane first, and believe me, no one tries to help THEM. They just let the helper fly off. The helper is the tragic hero. The sacrificial lamb. The helper always dies thirty seconds into the tragedy, it's documented.

Or I hear a cough. What if someone has an allergic reaction to peanuts? I don't recall this being a peanut-free zone. I don't even know CPR. I suppose I could fake it by punching people in the chest until the peanut popped out.

And then I want to know, when does the helping end? If the plane crashes into the sea or on a desert island, am I still the designated helper? Just exactly when does my helping contract expire? Will I be forced to cook 175 coconut meals for everyone in coach until a Russian tuna boat pops up? At what point am I free from my helping obligations?

You know, that's it. Why can't I just lie? That's totally what I'm going to do, just lie. Yeah. If I hear someone yell, "Help Girl! Help Girl! Get the Help Girl!" I'm just going to say, "Don't look at me, I lied. I will not Help, I have no Help to give. I'm just here for the leg room and the free drinks."

It was at that point that I saw the flight attendant pass, and I waved at her, determined to get this thing settled. "Do people ever...say 'no' to helping?" I asked.

"Of course," she said. "People with bad backs or selfish, bad people. If you're the helper and we have to evacuate, you get to be the first one down the slide."

"Oh," I said. "There's a slide? I didn't know about the slide."

The flight attendant leaned forward and smiled. "Oh yes. A big yellow one that inflates. It's very puffy."

"Wow, I LOVE slides," I said. "and I LOVE helping!"

INVASION

I was staring into Vincent Van Gogh's fierce blue eyes.

The color of the sky, I was captivated by them, steady, unnerving, determined. I studied his nose, protruding, balled at the tip. I was amazed that after writing countless papers on and seeing this very same image in art history books all through college, I was standing in front of the real thing at the Los Angeles County Museum of Art. The wonder of it all got to me so thoroughly, the back of my neck started to feel hot.

And then it got hotter, and then it got hotter hotter hotter.

Usually, for me to get that excited, cream sauce and goat cheese have to be involved.

As I turned to investigate the source of the heat, I saw a short little man with the face of a goblin, standing very close and literally breathing down my neck. My friend Jamie, who was standing next to me, saw him, too.

"How's that body lice thing going?" she said to me loudly. "Got it under control yet?"

"I'm trying, but it means bathing EVERY DAY," I replied. "Don't come any closer, sister! Doc says they can jump three whole feet!"

My neck returned to its normal temperature as the goblin scurried away.

I'm pretty sure I already know what my last words are going to be, and it's a toss up between "Pass the salt" and "Would you please stop touching me!", though my money's on the latter. I need my space, and not in a metaphorical sense. I want, at all times, to be able to thrust my arms outward, twirl, and not touch a single thing, because that's my space and it belongs to ME. If people insist on breaching that respect, I can't help it; I'll just want to fight them, most preferably in a parking lot. One careless step from a stranger into my twirling circle, and it's all fists and elbows.

It's painfully obvious that some people have no knowledge of the personal space, thrust-and-twirl rule, especially in grocery lines, escalators and elevators. If I ever became president, the first thing I would do is set up boundaries and make it a law that if a stranger got closer than two feet from me in a grocery line, I could put them under citizen's arrest. Escalators would be painted with a green step and the words "Welcome," then a red step and the words "Back off, Creeper!", then another green step. The floors of elevators would be equipped with a grid, and if you stepped out of your square, you would be exiled to the stairs for forever, smoker or not.

I was standing in a grocery line yesterday and the man behind me was ill, his lungs rattling like a baby toy, and within a moment and he was on top of me, and every step I take to move away from him, he sees that as an invitation to follow. I hate people who tailgate, and these people are just the same, but they're bodygaters. I just wanted to turn around and say to him, "You know if I was a working girl, your tab would be $150 by now. Take one more step and I'm going to need to require a deposit."

I will admit that one of my fantasies is to enter a Wal-Mart with a cattle prod and shock people that violated my personal space. Bzzz. Bzzz. If I were in high school and said that, I'd probably be expelled and under constant observation by my school psychologist right now. But I don't want to hurt people, I just want to shock them a little, gently, gently. I want my personal space; I'm entitled to it. I don't see anything wrong with that.

I mean, what are these people thinking? Why do they want to be that close to a stranger? Why do they want to be that close to me? But Bzzz, and I have room to breathe until the next cow comes along.

I had a party once when a friend brought a guest who upon meeting me, held my hand for a half an hour while her eyes rolled around like a pin ball in her head. It was horribly uncomfortable, and I was at a loss as to what to do. Now I know. Bzzz. She won't make that mistake twice, and if she does, then I get to tag her ear.

At the museum, things were getting increasingly worse.

"Unbelievable," Jamie said as we moved on to the next Van Gogh painting as the exhibit began to fill up. "It's a scientific fact that people shouldn't be that close to one another. I heard about this experiment where scientists put a bunch of deer on an island and it got too crowded and they all DIED. When places get overpopulated, you stop flourishing!"

"He was BREATHING on me," I informed her. "Breath that came from inside his body, and frankly, I don't want to come into contact with ANYTHING from inside anyone else's body!"

"It's a biohazard, plain and simple," she said as we passed by another painting, and I believed her because she's a microbiologist. "It's nothing but exhaust! Germ-wise, your butt won't get people as sick as your mouth will."

That was not good news, since it was apparent that the museum had sold tickets to 600 other people for the same time slot we had. The steady stream of people showed no indication of slowing, and they were ALL breathing. Inside the four rooms of Van Gogh paintings, it was getting as crowded as a Dillard's shoe sale as people came at us from all angles, fighting for the best view of the artwork. Soon, we were but two faces in a sea of steaming, open, germ-filled mouths.

I tried to keep my space by taking tiny steps away from other folks, but then they would take a tiny step, too, not understanding that my tiny step was not the "Oh Look, We're Moving Ahead" step but the "Get Away From Me Before I File Sexual Harassment Charges Against You" step. One fellow got so close to me that I wanted to ask him if any of my moles had changed colors. The rooms were getting more and more crowded, people were getting closer and closer until I felt like I was 11 years old again, stuffed in the backseat of the Country Squire station wagon, screaming at the top of my lungs, "THEY'RE ALL TOUCHING ME!!!!!"

More and more people crowded in to admire the art, and I clung to Jamie as the crowd pushed the two of us together so closely we briefly considered dating. In front of the painting of Van Gogh's bedroom, someone helped themselves to a handful of Jamie's butt, and I saw her scream as the tangle of bodies picked me up and carried me to another room.

"I'm not flourishing!" I yelled to her as we lost grasp on each other. "I'm definitely not flourishing!"

She looked me in the eye and raised her fist as the wave carried me farther out. "Don't forget!" she pronounced over the crowd. "Thrust and Twirl! Don't let history forget!"

Before I knew it, the mob had dumped me in the Van Gogh Mall, which was supposed to be a gift shop at the end of the exhibit. If I thought people were behaving badly while trying to get their five seconds in front of a Van Gogh masterpiece, the true horror didn't unveil itself until the element of merchandise was introduced. Though I had the opportunity to purchase an empty absinthe set for $70.00, a magnet for ten, or a watch with the face of painting Jamie's butt was fondled in front of for $60, I quickly snatched up a catalog and figured that since I had barely seen any of the paintings, I might as well start forming fake memories from the pictures.

I was getting ready to buy the catalog when Jamie got spit out of the crowd at the entrance to the mall.

"I was socked in the gut by an old man, pinched on the arm by a lady and a strange child grabbed my boob," she said as she came toward me, and suddenly her expression changed from relief to total alarm.

I was about to ask her what was wrong when my neck got very, very hot.

I was Butter Shamed at Costco today. You get four pounds for $10, so I bought sixteen pounds of butter **BECAUSE I HATE GOING TO COSTCO.** On the way out, the old, skinny receipt checker said, "That sure is a lot of butter." I said, "Out there in the real world butter is $5 a pound now. Of course I'm going to stock up." Then she said (snottily), "I never use butter," and I replied (snottily), "Then you're probably going to get cancer."

IS THAT YOUR BOYFRIEND?

It was my husband who saw it first.

"Hey," he said, leaning toward the TV, "Isn't that your old boyfriend?"

It's a question he asks me a lot, especially if he's watching COPS or *America's Most Wanted*.

"I told you, just because some guy on the news walks out of a trailer without a shirt on, has a beer in his hand and is being questioned by the police doesn't mean I've dated him," I shouted from the kitchen.

"I think this is the guy who had the snakes," he yelled back.

A thin shiver coiled up my spine. The snakes. I even pretended that I liked the snake, named (I'm embarrassed to say this part) Sid Vicious, a 13-foot reticulated python, that lived in a glass cage the size of a John F. Long home, minus the do-it-yourself "add-on."

Quickly, I learned to hate Sid, even though this was during the mid 80s and boyfriends with snakes were just part of the deal. I understand the food chain and the order of nature, but actually witnessing a fat, sluggish reptile attack an ordinary field mouse was more than I could stomach. It very easily could be equated to the terrifying vision of Linda Tripp ripping into a deli ham on rye.

I was especially horrified when Mary, a small white mouse I had named after the blind, pretty sister on Little House on the Prairie, was in the process of being digested. She had bravely managed to survive for nearly two weeks, hiding in a hollow knot of the tree branch that rested in Sid's cage. I really thought she was going to make it, she was very quick, and managed to roam freely about the cage without catching the snake's attention. I was devastated when she was eaten, my black, liquid eyeliner running down my cheeks.

"She went down in two bites," he said as softly as he could. "Will you help me shave my head now?"

"This is just so totally sad," I persisted, sobbing.

"Man, I told you, you gotta quit naming them, dude," he said, nodding.

"I am so not a dude," I said, reminding him.

He kept nodding.

In the middle of summer, the boyfriend came home with 13 rats in box. "I'm gonna breed 'em," he insisted, and I just turned away as he placed all of them in an aquarium in the bedroom closet. That night, I had a nightmare that my mom was scratching at the window, and when I woke up, I realized that it was only the sound of the closet rats tearing up the newspaper in the aquarium, and made the boyfriend move them to the laundry room.

The next morning, I entered the kitchen just as the boyfriend was on his fifth trip to the trash can, holding a limp rat by the tail. "There's no vent in here!" he said, standing in front of the dryer and the steamed-up aquarium. "Six of them are dead!"

I looked at the remaining seven rats. "Ma and Pa are gone," I cried hysterically. "So are Carrie, Almanzo and Mary The Second!"

The boyfriend put the rats outside in the carport to give them some air, but then promptly forgot about them after a meeting with his bong. By the time he remembered, the sun had shifted and had raised completely over head, causing a magnifying glass and ant type of scenario within the aquarium. I couldn't look bring myself to look as Laura, Nellie and Miss Beadle met the fate of their previously expired friends.

My hate was sealed and delivered one night as I was walking down the dark hall and something batted me in the head and I saw something waving in mid air, like the trunk of a circus elephant. I immediately flipped the light switch, and that's when I saw the first six feet of Sid, whipping around like a firehouse four feet off the ground. The snake had managed to escape from the cage, had squeezed through a tiny space in between the door jamb and a bedroom door and trying to free itself. The boyfriend solved the problem by taking and ax and a crowbar to the door jamb, trashing the dream of getting our security deposit back.

My aversion to reptiles of all sorts was dully confirmed several years later when a hippie suddenly put a four-foot iguana on my head one night at Long Wong's. My head quickly bowed under the 15-pound weight of the lizard, but when the hippie tried to remove his scaly pal, the iguana dug it's claws into my scalp and refused to budge. For forty-five minutes, the hippie and three of my friends each took a leg and worked non-stop to get the lizard off, creating a slight commotion as 30 onlookers watched, including my then-current boyfriend (the snake boyfriend and I broke up when he got an underage girl pregnant). Finally, the animal pooped on my head and relaxed enough to release its claws, but I couldn't move my neck for a week, was forced to wash my hair repeatedly with liquid Tide and my then-current boyfriend dumped me for the girlfriend of the hippie, who ran off together for Oregon in a van.

I was thinking about that when my husband called again from the living room. "Hurry!" he shouted. "This guy on TV has a snake tattoo on his neck, too! It's got to be him!"

"What did he do?" I asked, coming into the living room just before the news segment ended.

"He won the Powerball," my husband said. "Are you going to leave me?"

"Even though I'm sure he's bought a triple-wide mobile home, a hydroponics system and a big screen TV by now," I assured him, "That thing on his neck wasn't a tattoo. It was moving all on its own."

"The front door to their trailer looked like someone had attacked it with an ax," my husband added.

"I bet it did," I answered.

LOST

The streets were getting darker, and it wasn't my imagination.
I suddenly realized how quickly situations can change.
A mere eight minutes before, we had been jolly, happy tourists in Seattle, heading back to our hotel after eating dinner with friends.

Now, we were lost at 11:07 p.m. in a strange city and I was angry.

Don't get me wrong. I love Seattle. It's a beautiful place, though I can't help but feel suspicious of a city that can't be troubled to mark the exits of their freeways. They just pop up. There are no signs, no warning, and what's even worse, the exit can be on either side of you, right or left. You never know.

This is precisely where we as navigators— armed with three maps and directions delivered by our aforementioned friends—messed up as firm believers in logic.

It happened like this: we passed the Space Needle, and then, two seconds later, we were in a deserted railroad yard.

"What..." I said to my husband, who was commanding the wheel as I looked around at our blackened, barely-lit surroundings.
"How...when...*where* are we? Did I miss something? Weren't were just on the freeway! Where is the freeway?"

"Check the map," my husband said calmly.

"How did we end up here?" I questioned, searching the distance for the lights of downtown. "Do you think we just experienced...missing time?"

"Honey, just check the map," my husband repeated.

"The map won't help us," I announced. "We've been abducted. That is the only logical explanations. Freeways don't just END. What if I've been implanted with alien embryos? It's a good tax deduction, but *still*. Are you okay?"

"Just check the MAP!" he said sternly.

"It's okay if they messed with your butt, honey," I said as gently as I could. "I think I can love you anyway."

"Wait!" he said pointing off to the distance. "Is that the Space Needle?"

"Drive toward it!" I yelled as my husband took a right turn, which suddenly, and without explanation, took us right back on the freeway.

I took a deep breath and sunk back into the seat of the rental car.

We were about to be safe.

We continued on the freeway with the Space Needle fully in view and were getting closer to it, closer, closer, closer, almost there, when suddenly, the freeway dipped and turned and our view was gone.

The Space Needle had evaporated precisely at 11:18 p.m. without so much as a hint.

And, with just as much warning, we suddenly learned that we were a couple of tourists discovering the sights and pleasures of the seedier side of Seattle which made the railroad yard look like a Comfort Inn.

As we rolled down the streets in our rented car, my mouth fell open as I stared out the window.

"This looks just like the opening scenes from *Welcome Back, Kotter*," I said quietly as we passed a burned out car sitting in a vacant lot. "And I can tell you right now that there's no place on that map that's marked 'The Big Dirty Ghetto.'"

We were targets, I knew that. I knew that because we were driving the Bull's Eye. At the rental car counter I jumped at the chance to get a sport utility vehicle over a Dodge Neon for an extra five bucks a day. That was my decision, a genius idea from Miss Fancy Pants. And now, driving in the middle of Shantytown, people grouped on corners were looking at us as if it was gonna cost us a whole lot more.

I'll admit it. I was scared. Really, really scared. Of all the stupid ways to die, I thought to myself, by getting lost in a brand new Isuzu Rodeo that's costing me $40.95 a day, plus 18 percent tourist tax to finance Seattle's new sport stadium that has already killed more construction workers than the Bank One Ballpark did. I can't even be murdered for something that I own. I'm going to die as a Yuppie poseur, an affluent wannabe, and that's almost worse than dying naked. There is simply no dignity in dying for a rental car, and there aren't very many more ways to die that are dumber. I mean, *really*. I once knew a guy who killed a bicyclist by stopping too short at an intersection and whacked the bike rider on the back of the head with the passenger side mirror. Talk about senseless. I always figured that's the way I would go, in a moronic freak accident in which my husband drops his electric razor on the floor, it comes in contact with my my pinkie toe that happens to be in a dime-sized puddle of water and my fat immediately liquefies and fries me like a pork rind.

At least I won't die alone, I guess there's some solace in that. Mr. Magoo will be with me. I always prayed that I wouldn't die alone at home, not because that's sad, but because our maniacal puppy is the kind of dog who wouldn't wait until I exhaled my last breath before she took the first chunk out of my calf, and there I'd be, eaten alive by a dog that barks at her own doody.

For five dollars less a day, we'd be fine right now. No one would be pointing at us, staring at us or yelling at us. You'd feel too sorry for someone that drove a Neon to kill them. And, if we die here, at least I've beat the predictions of my mother, who swore that I'd perish while vigorously picking my nose and subsequently puncturing my brain with something sharp.

"I always kind of liked being Mrs. Magoo," I confided to my husband, figuring that in our final moments, I should come clean.

"Well, what you don't realize about Mr. Magoo," he replied, keeping his eyes on the road, "Is that in the end, he always comes out okay."

I nodded patronizingly, but just as I looked up, as we sped forward and the valley of old, tall buildings began to open, I saw the unmistakable red neon light of our hotel right in front of us.

"Wow," I said in amazement. "That was pretty smooth, even for an alien abduction."

Dad Dropped and Killed Holiday Sasquatch. Surgery in Progress.

Lunch With Mom

"How long is this going to take?" my mother said as she sat down at the table. "I'm missing a very good show on QVC by having lunch with you."

I took a deep breath.

Due to several nasty pieces of reader mail I received, I thought it might be a good idea to have a New Little Buddy contest. Based on the advice of my Nana, I decided to have readers vote for which hate letter writer you thought I should take to lunch and make my new best friend, or at the very least, a chance to beat up a rude person.

To everyone's surprise, including mine, the number of votes casted for each hate mail writer didn't even come close how many votes the winner, a write-in candidate, had.

That was my mom.

And now, true to my word, I was taking the victor out to lunch, even though I knew it was prime time for her to bug me about the menu of things she lives to bug me about. Although some subjects change seasonally ("Do you still have that pimple on your neck?", "When are you going to return my Tupperware?", "You're going to be on time for Thanksgiving, aren't you, because don't be surprised if you get here and we've already eaten"), she also has a schedule of regular items. These find their way into every conversation and consist of "When are you going to make an appointment for the gynecologist?" "Is your house clean or is it still filthy?" "You're not smoking, are you?" and "When are you going to be in a better mood?"

"You don't need to borrow money, do you?" my mother began by asking, which is an alternate selection. "Is that why you asked me to lunch? A lunch that I have a psychic premonition I'm going to end up paying for."

"Here is my Visa card, Mom," I said, pulling it out of my wallet. "I am planning on using this to pay for your lunch, just as long as the total bill does not exceed $15.81. For the tip, I have five dollars in rolled pennies that Nana forgot in my car after I took her to get a perm. It's not stealing, she owed me gas money anyway."

My mother rolled her eyes.

This is my mom. In those rolling eyes, I will never be an adult. Never. I have a mortgage. I have a husband. I kind of, sort of have a job. To my mom, however, I'm still the sixth-grader that she made get undressed in a dressing room with an 80-year old bra saleswoman at Sears when my "lentils" started to become "pintos." I know I am still that sixth-grader because she did it again three years ago when I was shopping for a wedding dress. I was 30 and she made me get naked in that dressing room with a stranger after she wormed her finger into my right armpit to make sure I "didn't go in there unshaven like an animal." Honestly, there was nothing I could do about it then, and if it happened today, I'd still be helpless. According to my mother, child abuse wasn't illegal until the 1980's, so under the grandfather clause, she can still whip off her shoe and hit me with it at any given time without consequence.

"How's your husband who broke your middle finger?" she said, taking a forkful of lunch. "Pass the salt."

"See? This is pal talk," I replied after taking a bite. "This is good. Well, Little Buddy, it finally happened. I had to ban him from making ice cubes. He only fills up the tray halfway with water, which doesn't really make ice *cubes*, it makes ice *disks*. Not only is it impossible for me to get my fingernail positioned correctly to lift up the disk, but it takes half a tray to fill up a glass. Would you pass the salt?"

"And you wonder why you have a broken finger. Why didn't we go to the Camelback Inn?" my mother asked. "This place is awful. Pass the salt."

"Look," I said, holding it up. "It's all deformed and useless. It doesn't even look like a finger anymore. It's like a claw. Pass the salt."

"You get a real kick out of doing that, don't you?" my mother said, shaking her fork at me. "That's a sin, you know, sin you wear like it's a fur coat! Did you make an appointment for the gynecologist yet? Pass the salt."

"Well," I said quietly, "I have been having that...not-so-fresh feeling..."

"I'm *eating,* for Christ's sake!" she said as she shot me a look. "No porno talk when I have food in my mouth, all right? That's disgusting."

"How's your blood pressure?" I replied. "I see a vein in your neck that's pulsing out the rhythm to La Vida Loca."

"How are you doing with the smoking?" she volleyed back at me as she pushed her plate away. "And don't tell me that you quit, because your head smells like a big round ashtray!"

"It's not me, Mom," started, taking a big breath, "It's sitting in all of those AA meetings. Did *you* go to the gynecologist yet?"

"Get that picture out of your head!" she hissed as the waiter took our dishes. "You should be more worried about the fact that you haven't been to the dentist in two years! I'm amazed that you don't spit out little bullets of teeth when you talk. Your mouth is as clean as your house. Filthy!"

"I only have one good hand!" I protested, holding up my bandaged digit. "I can barely wipe myself!"

"Excuse me," the waiter jutted in quietly. "Do you have another card, because," and then he whispered this part, "this one's been... 'used up'."

"I should start my own hotline, like Jackie Stallone," my mother said wryly as she dug for her Visa. "I told you I had a vision."

"Read my mind now, Mom," I said.

She looked at me.

"I'm wearing flip-flops," she warned. "I can have them off faster than you can say, 'Mommy don't hit me!'"

"Mo—" I started.

"Lay off the salt," she said, looking at me closely as she put her shoe back on. "It's not a vitamin, you know. Your face is all puffed up like a water balloon."

I learned it by watching you, okay! I replied. "Do you think maybe we could get some diuretics on QVC?"

"You can get *God* on QVC," my mother said. "Come over. I'll even put it on my credit card. Quit rubbing your arm. I didn't hit you that hard."

"And, on the third day, he hath risen."
-- 14:1, Book of Squatch.

PLEASE RING

The phone rang, loud and shrill. I picked it up on the first ring, which was simple since I had been hovering over the phone for the last hour. Staring at it. Talking to it, coaxing it to ring.

"Please ring," I thought, whimpering in my mind. "I'm so hungry."

It was Memorial Day, a day of parades, flying flags, an extra day off from work and barbecues. Hot dogs, soft drinks and chips and dips go on sale. But for my husband and I, the holiday caught us last year in the thin, struggling days before the second payday of the month was due to arrive.

Earlier in the day, we had planned on a picnic, but after my husband has scoured the cabinets and refrigerator for goodies, he turned to me in utter dismay.

"Are you Mother Hubbard?" he asked. "There's nothing in here but a lemon and a bowl of something furry that looks like it's grown teeth."

"We could still go on a picnic," I offered. "Maybe we could steal food from ducks at the park."

"If you want to wrestle a chicken bone from a rabid duck at the park, that's your business," he said. "I'll just get a hammer and kill what's in that bowl for lunch."

"I'd use the shovel," I said. "Hey, maybe someone will call and invite us over for a barbecue!"

Someone HAD to invite us over. We had some upwardly mobile friends with gas grills as big as cars, and even though we considered them show-offs, we were hungry enough to eat food off of anyone's table. So there I sat as the morning progressed, my eyes glued to the phone, my mind exercising a Jedi Mind Trick to get it to ring. On the first jingle, I snatched up the receiver. It was my mother, who certainly, in a motherly fashion, would provide sustenance for her starving brood.

"Are you having a barbecue?" I asked immediately. "Because we'll come over."

"No," she answered. "We're going to Sedona for the day. I just wanted to call and remind you to take down your Christmas tree."

"You said that yesterday," I informed her. "I told you it still looks pretty."

"Dried-up trees can spontaneously combust, you know," she replied before hanging up. "Skin grafts don't look so nice, even on a married girl."

Exasperated, I flicked on the television and retired to the couch, where I watched Bob Villa tour a toilet bowl factory. On the first commercial, a group of friends gathered around a gas grill and watched brats get plump and juicy, turning a delicious shade of chocolate brown. During the second commercial, several women discussed feminine hygiene products while they drank coffee and ate scones. In the third commercial, an irrational, manic-depressive black poodle whined for a can of Mighty Dog, which looked pretty good once it got branded. By the time Bob was back at the factory, inspecting the streamlined beauty of a bidet, my mouth was watering.

"I want brats! And scones!" I shouted to my husband, who was now searching for the blow torch. "How much money do you have?"

"I have three dollars," he answered from the hall closet.

I found my purse and emptied my wallet, finding only an old coupon for Yonique, the Yogurt You Drink wrapped around a used piece of chewing gum and a sample strip of Biore. Then I hit gold.

"We're saved!" I sang loudly. "I've found the credit card! I don't think this one has been canceled yet!"

"I'll give it a shot," my brave husband offered. "I'll go to the store, and you stay here and man the phone!"

"Get some Mighty Dog!" I shouted as he pulled out of the driveway.

He hadn't even reached our street corner when the phone rang. "May I speak to Laurie Notaro?" the voice on the other end of the phone requested.

Oooo, a formal barbecue, I thought. Maybe they'll have deviled eggs or a cheese log. "This is she," I said gleefully.

"This is Mrs. Watson from Citibank," the voice said. "We're scheduled to close your account unless we receive immediate payment with an electronic money transfer."

"It's Memorial Day," I stammered. "You're not supposed to be calling on a holiday!"

"I'm a slave to corporate America, ma'am," she answered.

My mind raced with ideas to stall her long enough for my husband to get to the store, pick up the brats and get to the cashier before I was launched into credit card purgatory.

"How long to you typically leave your Christmas tree up?" I asked her. "Have you ever had or known of one to spontaneously combust?"

"I have a fake tree, ma'am," she answered.

When my husband returned home with a grocery bag in hand, I jumped and screamed with happiness as if I had found a mouse in a can of Dr. Pepper and had grounds to sue for monetary reparations.

He, on the other hand, didn't look so happy. He tossed the credit card on the counter in complete defeat and shook his head. "They got to us," he offered simply.

"I tried to stall her, I really did," I cried. "I got her to tell me about her alcoholic aunt that suddenly burst into flames while smoking a cigarette and watching a Gene Hackman movie. There was nothing left of her but a little pile of white ash and her Easy Spirit shoes!"

"What?" my husband said, still shaking his head.

"Looks like a pump, feels like a sneaker?" I prompted. "Well, then what's in the bag?"

He handed it to me, and as I opened it, my heart dropped. Tucked inside the bag was an eight-pack of Corn Boy fat-free hot dogs past the expiration date and two cans of Slim-Fast.

"With three bucks, that's the closest thing I could afford to brats," he explained. "After we get sick on the hot dogs, the Slim-Fast will fill us up."

"But we don't have rolls," I whimpered.

"Hot Dog Soup," he boasted proudly. "We cut up the hot dogs, boil them, and pour it all into a bowl."

"I'd rather eat my own hair," I said with recoil.

"You might want to save your hair," he replied. "I'm thinking for my birthday I might want a watch. I did notice about twenty cars parked in front of a house around the corner, and I saw barbeque smoke coming from the backyard."

"Twenty cars, huh?" I said, thinking. "Maybe we wouldn't be noticed."

"Put your walking shoes on," he said, with an impish grin, and then I heard his stomach growl.

THEY DON'T CARE

Naughty or nice.
    Naughty or nice.
    It looked like I had a decision to make.
    I faltered with it, back and forth, as I approached the line at the checkout as it grew, exponentially, by the second.
    If you've ever been to a do-it-yourself craft store in the weeks preceding the holiday season, I can fully confirm that you have experienced the seventh circle of Hell.
    All I needed was a $1.49 chunky rubber stamp, and found myself fourth in line, right behind a lady with dyed ratty hair. Despite the two cashier's stations facing each other, some genius had decided that we were all going to form one line, which stretched out into the aisle and placed me in front of a rack of twinkle light nets on sale for $2.99. After the third Glue Gun Queen grazed my shin with her cart and caught the bottom of my back pack purse with her elbow, I turned around and bellowed a loud EXCUSE ME, just to prove that I hadn't taken my invisible pills that morning.
    Oh, the cart wielding maniac giggled. "Those back packs are so cute, but they can be such a pain sometimes!"
    "Yeah," I agreed, flashing my gummiest, widest smile. "Though it generally isn't bothersome until someone tries to ram a cart up my butt. You can go ahead and try it, but I'd have to charge you my standard rate unless you have a military ID."
    It was starting to get pretty hot in the store. At one of the registers, a couple was arguing with the cashier about a seven-foot fake Christmas tree that had been advertised but had sold out; at the other register, a woman who had gone to high school with Mary Todd Lincoln moved up to the counter with a wagon full of 29-cent stems of gold and red silk flowers.
    "Twenty-nine, twenty-nine, twenty-nine," the cashier announced as she scanned each tag.

"No!" the silk flower woman crackled. "That one was from the twenty-five cents cart!"

"I bet the last time you were behind a cart it was being pulled by oxen," I said under my breath.

"Twenty-nine, twenty-nine, twenty-nine..."

Suddenly, from the corner of my eye, I saw something suspicious, something miraculous. A man in a craft-store apron was moving slowly behind another register, and with his hairy hand, he reached over and flipped on his open light.

I don't think you could have gotten a bunch of women to move quicker than if someone had announced, "The Snackwell Ladies are here with free cookies!" Before I could even move to that line, however, the women behind me executed a cut-off, and changed lanes without even signaling.

The rat haired woman and I gasped together.

"That's not fair!" she shouted. "Nine people behind us just got in that line! We were here first! He didn't take the next person in line!"

"The cashiers don't care," I said drolly. "The same thing happened the last time I was here."

"Really?" the rat-haired woman said as I nodded. Then she raised her little rat head above the crowd, shot the new cashier a dirty look and yelled, "Hey YOU! Cashier man! We were here first! You didn't even ask who was next in line!"

"What do you want me to do?" the male cashier asked harshly. "Do you want me to stop helping this lady and help you instead?"

The rat woman thought for a moment and then looked him straight in the eye. "YES," she retorted. "YES I DO."

"Twenty-ni—"

A hush fell over the whole store and everyone just stared as the rat haired woman made her way through the congestion to the front of the new line and plopped her stuff on the counter, never once dropping her head, never once unlocking her little red eyes from those of the cashier.

Sally Field couldn't have done it better. I felt like clapping and throwing long-stemmed roses at her.

"Forty dollars and sixty cents is NOT right!" the silk flower lady yelled to her cashier, her shaky finger pointing. "I had it all figured out on paper this morning! You're trying to cheat me!"

The fake seven-foot-tall Christmas tree-arguing couple marched out of the store, and the line moved forward and the woman in front of me took her place at the check-out. Only purchasing several boxes of string lights, the transaction was smooth, easy and almost over.

"I will not be cheated!" the old silk-flower woman yelled. "We're going to count these together and then you'll see what a cheat you are!"

The lady at the other check-out was signing her name to her check. It was almost over. Almost over if I could just hang on, although I could feel an attack of Mall Malice—Road Rage's bitter little sister—coming on, and I very badly wanted to pinch somebody.

"And here's your receipt," the cashier smiled pleasantly to the light lady, handing her the piece of paper. I took a step forward, anxious, waiting. I was teetering on anticipation.

"I want you to plug in these lights to see if they work," the lady said as she took the receipt.

I wasn't sure if I heard her right, but then understood that I had as she opened the package of lights and fished around for the cord.

I believe it was at this moment that I fell off the teeter-totter, that I lost whatever grasp I had on what was left of my patience, and my pinching fingers began twitching.

Naughty, naughty.

"NO WAY," I heard myself freak out. "No way. NO. You are not plugging in those lights. You DO NOT get to do that," and then to the cashier, "She is not plugging in those lights," and to the crowd of angry women behind me, "She wants to plug in the lights!!!"

"I don't have an outlet," the cashier offered.

"But I want to see if they work," the light woman insisted.

"I don't get to test out this stamp before I buy it," I bellowed as I held up my item, then pointed to the woman behind me. "She doesn't get to try out her paint. Those are the rules."

The light woman just looked at me, holding the cord in her hand.

I stood there, holding my stamp in mine.

Naughty or nice.

I turned around, put the stamp down on the closest shelf and walked out of the store.

Then I drove to another craft store clear across town.

As I was standing eighth in the check-out line with another stamp in my hand, the cashier one register over flicked on her light and a thousand women guided by glue guns descended upon her like she was a naked grapevine wreath.

"That's not fair!" the woman behind me said. "She didn't take the next person in line!"

"The cashiers don't care," I said drolly. "The same thing happened the last time I was at one of these stores."

My dad was just watching Bill O'Reilly's series on Fox about the wild west that I honestly mistook for Drunk History.

GET A NIGHT JOB

My husband snores.
Loudly.
    In the deep throes of slumber, the man I married sounded remarkably like a pig chowing down at a trough. Actually, let's make that a herd of pigs. The sound was so loud it puts the expression "sawing logs" to shame, as every night, my husband depleted an entire redwood forest with a jackhammer before he woke.
    Sadly, however, I was already awake. At the very moment when I was about to slip into the dream land where I become a size eight or the first female cappo in the Soprano family, a snorting equivalent to a sonic boom reached out and jolted me awake.
    I tried to be kind. I bought two sizes of those little nose anti-snoring strips: large, to help my husband decrease his snoring, and medium for me as a sympathetic gesture and also because I thought if something was taping my skin in place for a steady eight hours I could possibly avoid asking for a jowl tuck as a birthday gift. The nose strips, however, proved remarkably ineffective as my husband's snorting bursts *still* woke me up and also because I was getting freaked out when I began waking up and they were no longer holding up my excess skin, mainly because they were no longer there.
    Terrified that my body was misidentifying the sticky nose strips as a carbohydrate and immediately absorbing them, I began panicking until I woke up one morning with restricted sight and I started to cry about being half-blind until I realized a sticky nose strip was taping my eye shut. A further investigation revealed about 14 sticky nose strips stuck to the headboard behind my pillow, so I came to the conclusion that Sleeping Laurie doesn't like nose strips, removes them and then *puts* them places.
    My husband, however, is not as sympathetic as I am. I bought him sticky nose strips, and he bought me a pair of earplugs and suggested

that I get a night job. But over the weekend, I saw a news show that gave tips to stop my husband from snoring. While there is no miracle cure, the newscaster said, it helps if you stop smoking, don't eat or drink five hours before you go to bed, lose weight or sew a tennis ball to the back of your pajamas to force you to sleep on your side.

Or I could get a night job.

I decided that the only viable option was the tennis ball, but how exactly would anyone sew a tennis ball to the back of a pajama top? I looked for a tennis ball setting on my sewing machine (oddly enough, mine can only sew racquetballs), and even if I sewed it by hand, once I put the needle into the ball, I'd need Yuri Geller to get it back out. I thought maybe I could Velcro the tennis ball, I could maybe staple it, I could glue it, or make something of a pocket womb for it. But I decided not to do any of that.

"I want my own bedroom," I announced one night at dinner. "Your snoring is keeping me awake, and I'm so tired that some people at work said that I was drunk!"

"Oh, here we go again," my husband said, throwing up his hands. "No, you cannot have your own bedroom, just like you cannot have your own refrigerator, your own couch or imminent domain status over the bathroom! We are MARRIED! We share things!"

"That is so unfair," I pouted. "I should tape record you snoring to show you how unfair you are!"

Later that night, I smuggled my hand-held recorder under the sheets with me. Apparently, however, I was so tired that I dozed off before my husband came to bed and I had a chance to tape him. I woke up the next morning, however, to the sound of a herd of hungry pigs and the tape recorder inches from my face as my husband held it.

"See?" I demanded groggily, figuring that I must have rolled over on the tape recorder and luckily pushed the right button. "See? Who can sleep through that? It sounds like someone is sucking your brain out through your nose with a straw! I demand my own room!"

"You got it, sister," my husband said with a wicked smile. "Because this isn't me. I found you drooling and snorting all over your recorder and decided to give you some of your own medicine. You've been waking yourself up, because this is *you* snoring, Wilbur!"

As I looked at him through my one sticky nose strip-free eye, I suddenly knew exactly what to do with that tennis ball.

NOW YOU SEE US, NOW YOU DON'T

"Are you done with that?" my Nana said a couple of weeks ago as she swept my plate out from underneath me with still half of a chicken cutlet on it.

"All through?" she said as she moved onto my sister, who was in the process of directing forkful of mashed potatoes into her mouth.

Nana quickly deposited the dishes into the sink, wiped her hands and said, "Well, thanks for coming by. It was nice to see you. Good bye!"

My sister and I looked at each other in silence. We have dinner at Nana's house every Wednesday night, but for the past couple of weeks, she had been giving us the boot before dinner was even over.

"Maybe she has a boyfriend," my sister whispered.

"Or a night job as an erotic dancer!" I shot back. "How dare you even think that filth about our Nana! Our Nana is so ... *Nana* that visions of her image appear to children in the French country side and on the sides of buildings in Mexico! So on my cue, we'll launch a joint attack to expose her intricate web of deceit!"

As Nana stood at the sink and waited for us to leave, I nodded to my sister and we moved in for the ambush.

"What's going on here?" I demanded. "Why are you so anxious to get rid of us?"

"I'm not anxious," our 98-pound Nana stuttered as my sister and I circled her like raptors. "I just need to clean some things!"

"This house is more sterile than an ICU unit," my sister said. "You could perform a kidney transplant right on the kitchen floor with no risk of infection!"

"No, there's a mess in the storage room," Nana carefully replied. "All the stuff that Pop Pop saved. Yesterday I threw away a whole stack of newspapers with headlines like, 'Pearl Harbor Bombed,' 'Lindbergh Flies Around World' and 'Men Walk on Moon'! Now who needs newspapers like that? It's not *news anymore*! We already know what happened!"

"I think I just heard the sound of a grave being rolled around in," I said.

"Talking about it just makes me want to clean more," Nana said quickly as she looked at the clock. "I spotted some Civil War junk on the back shelf! Those guns are so old I bet they don't even work! Now go home, the both of you!"

"OK, Nana," I said harshly. "Have it your way. Let's see how tough you are when I throw this right-from-the-box Entemann's coffee cake on this clean floor of yours!"

"Oh, don't! It's not even past the freshness date!" Nana cried as her hands flew to her face. "All right! All right! My show is going to be on tonight for the last time and I wanted to watch it in peace!"

"But *JAG* is on tomorrow night," my sister said curiously.

"That's NOT my favorite show," Nana snipped.

"What's on Wednesdays?" I said in a panic to my sister. "On, no! Please tell me it's not *90210*, Nana! I don't want to have to put you in a home!"

"No, no, no, I don't watch that stupid show. My show is called *Beverly Hills, Now You See Us, Now You Don't*. Donna's getting married tonight," Nana continued. "And I just have to see how they shove her croquet-ball boobs into a wedding dress! Sometimes she's so slutty!"

"Oh, dear Lord," I said in horror. "What other shows have you been watching in your secret life?"

"Well, I've always liked *An Angel is Touching Me*," she said as she paused to think. "But it just doesn't have the spunk of *Five People At A Party*."

"Nana's just like Mork and Mindy's baby!" I warned my sister. "She's going backward! I am telling you right now, old lady, I am NOT driving you to get your nipples pierced!"

"Oh, what those kids have been through on that show!" Nana sighed, shaking her head. "It's a shame, a real shame. Believe me, it's no party!!

Their parents died, one of the kids married a drug addict, another had a bastard baby, and now they have to sell the house because the show got canceled. Where are they going to go? What will they do? I don't know. I just don't know."

"Well, now that we know the truth about why you wanted us to leave," I said to Nana, "Please tell me that you were lying about those newspapers."

She shook her head adamantly. "No, it's true!" she protested. "Men really did walk on the moon. I saw it on TV, so you know it was real."

We have a day off from surgery stuff so we took a walk downtown and went into a hot chocolate place.
My dad: Do you guys take AmEx?
Hot Chocolate Girl: Yes.
My dad: Oh, good. I just found one outside on the sidewalk.
Lesson learned: Eighteen-year-old Hot Chocolate Girls do not understand my dad.

Nana's Bread

As soon as Nana and I pushed our shopping cart down the bread aisle, we could tell that there was something seriously wrong.
There, in the space on the top shelf that typically held loaves of Nana's favorite bread, was nothing.
Absolutely nothing.
My 83-year-old Nana clutched her beige vinyl purse to her chest and gasped.
"Where's my bread?" she cried, frantically scanning the shelves for the blue and white package. "My bread is GONE. MY BREAD IS GONE."
Sensing imminent danger, I quickly took control of the situation. As I rummaged through every loaf of bread on the top shelf, I felt a knot in my stomach grow.
"Nana," I said slowly, "It looks like they're all out of your bread."
Nana's mouth opened a little, the blood draining from her face, as a small, desperate, anguished wail leaked out from between her parted, blue lips.
"Oh my God," Nana said, shaking her head in disbelief. "I can't believe it. I can't believe it. What am I supposed to do now?"
There was no blue and white package to be found. Now, to anybody else, this would be far from a serious situation. You'd just pick another loaf of bread and move on. Most people don't have allegiances to a certain kind of bread, the occurrence would have as much detriment in it as if you had just discovered you'd married the wrong life partner. You'd just file some papers at the courthouse, then go to the bar and hook up with the first person who looked at you.
But Nana takes her bread very seriously. She's been eating the same kind of bread, a dense little loaf with VERY THIN slices but is still so sturdy I could tile my roof with them. She loves that bread.
"Is there another kind we can buy?" I asked, and judging by the look on her face, I had apparently vocalized the unthinkable. She looked at me as if I had just suggested she have a one-night stand with her high-blood

pressure doctor.

"My bread has a certain consistency!" she yelled. "It has a very nice taste to it. It's a solid piece, It's such a nice taste! Oh, God!"

On the way home, Nana just started out the window, not saying anything. After we unloaded and put away all of her other groceries, I waved as I pulled out of the driveway, calling, "See you on Sunday!"

"Yeah," she offered weakly. "If I last that long without eating toast."

I was determined to do whatever I could to secure Nana a supply of her bread. I traveled to every grocery store around my house to find it, and sent out an all-points bulletin to members of my family to keep an eye out for VERY THIN.

It was then that my sister that warned me of the dangerous ground I was treading on.

"Don't you remember The Great Sponge Expedition of 1996?" she asked me. "Remember when they stopped making Nana's favorite sponge and for the next two years, she bought a sponge at every store she went to until we realized they had just changed the packaging? And don't even get me started on The Impossible Cracker Hunt in the late 80's when we had to find a snack product that didn't gum up in her teeth. I had a better chance of finding a Bigfoot family nesting behind my pool pump."

Still, the next week, I took Nana shopping again, and the first place she wanted to hit was the bread aisle. Again, the VERY THIN slot was vacant.

"Why should I even bother getting up I the morning if I can't have my bread?" Nana wanted to know. "My life is going down the toilet! My mornings are so empty now, Kathie Lee is gone, and now my toast. Now I just sit there with coffee, no laughter, no toast. Oh, God, I tell you!"

I knew we had arrived at a desperate situation when I saw her assault a slice of Holsum bread by spraying it with water, taking a rolling pin to it and then trying to stuff it into the toaster slot.

I got on the Internet, found the bread manufacturer's website and e-mailed them a letter documenting the ferocity of the ordeal, including Nana's experiments with wet food and electricity. I asked them if I could buy direct from them, and was prepared to purchase a palate if need be.

But when I got a response back later that week, I felt like weeping myself.

"We are sorry to say that VERY THIN bread has been discontinued. Thank you for your interest."

Honestly, I couldn't bring myself to tell Nana. The shock would have been too great. She was already becoming withdrawn, had stopped eating any type of bread product altogether, and couldn't even look at a sandwich without turning her head away with tears in her eyes.

So I did the only thing I could do. I replied to the bread people, and this time, I shamelessly begged.

"Please start making Nana's bread again," I typed. "Otherwise, my Uncle Bill will have no choice but to sell all of his stock in your company. My Nana, Mrs. Bill Gates' Mom, would be so happy to have her toast again in the morning."

I wasn't surprised when they didn't answer me back, and the next time I took Nana to the store, and I felt guilty for feeding her false hope when she insisted on checking the bread aisle again.

"We can look," I said weakly. "But I wouldn't expect anything."

And then I heard Nana gasp. There, on the top shelf, was the familiar blue and white package of her favorite bread.

"My bread!" Nana cried as she lovingly cradled the first loaf I hauled down. "My bread! God answered my prayers!"

"I am so happy," Nana continued, the joy on her face barely contained. "Now if I could just find a damn cracker that didn't turn into glue as soon as I do you mind if we check the snack aisle?"

Had a dream that my favorite restaurant had a Spanx Night....All you had to do was snap your waistband for the waitress ands she gave you 25% off and dessert of your choice.

TAKE A SICK DAY, ASSHOLE

The noise came from somewhere behind me in the elevator yesterday. It was powerful and booming, full of force and strength. It rumbled toward the end, and commenced in a sharp, thin crack, consistent with a pair of contaminated pair of lungs brimming with vermin and disease.

It was a COUGH.

A big, foul, impure COUGH.

I spun around immediately, trying to detect the perpetrator in a chamber full of people. I scanned my eyes quickly among the faces, and then I found her.

She was easy to spot. With red, watery eyes and a shiny red sheen circling the orifices of her nose, the offender sheepishly looked away when my stare met hers, and then she coughed *again*.

I freaked out. I mean, there I was, trapped in a crammed, crowded elevator at work with a sick person and absolutely no means of escape. While her germs were busy flying around the tight space trying desperately to find a new host to land on and suck the life out of, it was everything I could do to pull my finger back from pounding on the emergency button. There was no place to go, nothing to do but wait as particles of disease fell on me like a rain shower.

I plugged my nose, held my breath and jumped off of that thing as soon as the doors opened. That's it, I thought as I climbed the four flights of stairs to my floor, that's it. Now I'm sick. In three days, I'll be all plugged up, dripping, wheezing, crabby, achy, hot, chilly, itchy, sweating, smelly and wanting to kill the person who did this to me.

At least I knew what my attacker looked like, I thought as I drew an artist's rendition of her face on my hand so I wouldn't forget, vowing to track her down and her snot trail as well. Why did she even come to work in the first place, I wondered. If you're sick, just stay at home. Let me tell you, if you come to work sick, you're not doing yourself any favors. It will destroy your popularity. No one will go to lunch with you, no one will talk to you without a surgical mask donning their face.

Around this time of year, the workplace is a breeding ground for disease and death, well, maybe not death, but if we were living in pioneer times, one sneeze was all it took to wipe out a whole village. One sniffle, and suddenly, orphans were wandering the countryside. Sitting at my desk, there's more danger of catching something than there is after a natural disaster with dead livestock floating around in my front yard. I'm sorry people are sick, but to tell you the truth, I'm not that sorry that I want to share their pain with them. Being sick is not the same thing as a good luck email. You don't need to spread it around to a hundred people to have the gods shine on you or get better. Keep your death rattle at home, I say, because I don't want it. In fact, I think making people stay at home when they're contagious should become a national policy. Being sick has the same properties as people who look at porn the Internet. Keep it where it belongs, in private. No one wants to know your secret. It will change the way we all look at you, it will gross us out, and you might even get a secret knick name, like "Infector Gadget."

For those folks who are absolutely determined to come to work with a box of tissues and Vicks VapoRub in their briefcases, well, they need to be prepared to pay the price. In my office, there's a running list, not quite Santa's list, of everyone who doesn't wash their hands when after go to the bathroom. Someone is keeping track. I'm not saying who, but he is a wise and precautions man and very well may end up saving countless lives. A select few of us know which bowls NOT to eat out of at the Friday potlucks, and I'm prepared to utilize the same kind of network here.

Black X's on doors, that's right, you come to work with a virus and I am prepared to out you. In fact, I don't even think that's going far enough. In my opinion, we need a quarantine unit set up for all of those selfish people who come to work when they're sick. You want to work so bad, go ahead. But it will be in a whole room of renegade nose-blowers and open-mouthed coughers who can infect each other repeatedly instead of contaminating the healthy population. If you sneeze once or twice, well, that happens, but more than that, it's the sick room for you. And when you're quarantined, you're *quarantined*. There will be a special sick restroom, complete with receptacles to dispose of your snot rags properly, like a bonfire. There will be a sick vending machine, outfitted with already contaminated buttons. I've seen sick people go through the lunch line at work, handling all the rolls and feeling up the fruit. No more! I witnessed one lady who made sure she touched every single cup within her arm's reach, then turned around and coughed like a coal miner.

I have to go now, because I have some work to do. I have only two days left to prepare my death bed on my living room couch, buy all of the orange juice I can before my debit card gets declined and get some big trash bags to hold all of my used tissues. Then, when I get better, I'm going to haul all of those biohazard waste bags to my office on my first day back at work, where one special elevator cougher will discover that her desk has suddenly become a Booger Float.

Holiday tip: when making a chocolate cheesecake and attempt to use a spoonful of sour cream for a design element, know that it's going to look like a bird shit on it.

OLD CHIGGER

From the corner of her cloudy eyes, she watched it as she crept up closer, slowly, slowly, she watched it, studied it, until she had zeroed in on it, opened her massive jaws and pounded her next meal.

"HEY! Drop it! *Drop it*!" I heard my husband yell, and I turned the corner just in time to see him engaged in a tug of war with our elderly dog, Chigger.

"What does she have now?" I asked, pointing to the object in Chigger's mouth that my husband was trying to wrench from her jaws. "Be careful, don't pull hard. We don't want any more of her teeth falling out!"

"She's eating the clicker!" he informed me. "She circled the coffee table six times and then attacked it like a shark!"

"I guess it kind of looks like a brownie, but be gentle," I reminded him. "TV remotes are easier to get than doggie dentures."

"It's not the TV remote!" he grunted. "It's the one for digital cable!"

That was enough to send me into a panic and consider running to get a chain to hook my husband to the bumper of my car.

Now, don't think that I don't love my dog, because both my husband and I completely adore her. It's just that her golden years have become something of a challenge for just about everyone involved. For instance, the digital cable remote wasn't the first indigestible object she attempted to recently eat. If its within her reach, if she can get her mouth around it and can stand up long enough to actually locate it, it's fair game. We've caught her red-handed trying to gulp down a hairbrush that we figured she mistook for a hot dog, a phone receiver she incorrectly identified as a burrito, and a bra that she mistook for Hostess Sno Balls, the remains of which I probably won't recover until after her autopsy.

Unless you've already had an older dog, you don't really know what to expect when your dog enters AARP status. At first, it's confusing. It's a whole new ball game. When her hearing went, we had to adapt, and started talking to her like she was a foreigner ("YOU NO PEE-PEE IN HOUSE! HOUSE NO PEE-PEE PLACE!"); when she could no longer see to catch a ball, we turned our heads and laughed so she wouldn't be ashamed. Of course, as time went on, new facets of the mature Chigger began to emerge. She developed new coping mechanisms, like time management strategies in which she would eat and relieve herself at once, or passed a silent killer when she wanted to be alone instead of getting up and moving to another room. It was just easier to stink us out. There was never any warning before she launched one, not a tummy rumble or a warning siren. If I could bottle that stuff, I tell you, I'd make a fortune selling it to the National Guard for dispersing riots or for refilling mace dispensers. With the threat of "toilette de Chigger" looming as a threat, the world would be a much calmer place, trust me on that one.

We also noticed that Chigger started becoming more forgetful, and sometimes she'd wake up and look around for a while until she realized where and who she was. My husband and I, however, decided to use this to our advantage and to enhance her life at the same time. We would take turns shaking her awake and exclaiming, "HOW YOU LIKE HAWAII? NOT ALL DOGS GO TO HAWAII! YOU SIT IN FIRST CLASS!", "YOU SO LUCKY TO LIVE WITH BRAD PITT AND JENNIFER ANISTON! YOU A LUCKY DOG!" and "THE DOG CONTEST PEOPLE JUST CALL! YOU WIN BEST IN SHOW, EVEN WITH BIG GROWTH ON YOUR HEAD!"

When she developed arthritis, we covered the floor with numerous rugs so that so our dog could walk instead of ice skate, although it severely took a chunk out of her entertainment value. As a result of her stiff joints, she's on enough drugs to be in a band and one night Robert Downey Jr. called for her. My husband says that when the times comes that she can't get around anymore, he'll build her a box that she can sit in with wheels on it, and I said okay, as long as we can attach a mop head to it. She still has to earn her keep, you know.

Still, it's odd to think of the puppy I brought home from the pound 14 years ago is so old that she wakes up sometimes and believes I'm Jennifer Aniston, but to be honest, if the whole world was 14 in dog years and thought the same thing, I couldn't complain. All I know is that every morning when I wake up, look over the side of the bed and see my dog open her eyes, all I can say is, "Right on, Chig! You're *alive!*" Frankly, I don't care to imagine a morning otherwise, even if I don't have to run out of the room screaming for air. See, she's my pal.

And that's sort of what I was thinking when my husband was wrestling

Chig for the digital cable remote, and I suddenly heard myself say, "Brad, let go. Let her have it. We can get another one."

After all, give an old dog a bone. Or remote. Or hairbrush. Or whatever.

That's what I was thinking. Well, that and, "Whew! I really need to buy some matches."

ON THE BEACH

The tops of my feet were so hot that I could have used them as a griddle and made grilled cheese sandwiches on them.

My friend Jamie said hers felt hot, too. I could already tell that by the way she hobbled off the Santa Monica beach the day before, her feet transformed in a matter of hours into bright crimson lobster claws. Mine didn't look much better, taking on the color of raw pork chops.

"Who really thinks of slapping sunscreen on your feet?", we both asked each other later that night as we packed our feet in ice.

"It's like putting sunscreen up your nostrils," she said.

"And we were careful with our sunscreen!" I agreed. "You can tell how good we were by the line right above our ankles where it's as white as Martha Stewart's sheets!"

"And by the silhouette of a pink naked lady on your neck because you didn't go all the way across!" Jamie added.

"I'm hungry!" I said. "Looking at my feet in ice is making me want a shrimp cocktail."

Looking at your neck makes is reminding me that I forgot to do my self breast exam this month! she informed me.

"This ruins *everything!*" I pouted. "I wanted one more day at the beach on my vacation!"

"On, no!" Jamie shouted. "We are going! We'll just have to wear a Beach Burn Victim's outfits for the ultimate in protection!"

The next morning, we arrived at the beach dressed like firefighters, complete with white, long sleeved shirts, pants, and sun hats bearing brims with the circumference of the rings around Jupiter. We parked our beach chairs close to the life guard's station for safety purposes, just in case a cookie or cheese and crackers were to get lodged in our throats, which would be a tragic beach disaster.

We covered our crab feet with towels and settled in for a nice picnic. The minute we broke out our salami sandwiches, however, a gang of seagulls landed around us in a perfect circle. One bird in particular took a fancy to me. Staring at my salami with two cold, beady eyes, he stood frozen in a pose. I took a bite of my sandwich and then looked at him again. He was a foot closer. I took nibbled on my cookie and glanced at the seagull. He was closer yet. After another bite of my sandwich, the seagull was closer still, in fact, he was standing on my protective burned foot towel.

"Go away!" I shouted, trying to wave the bird off, but he wasn't going anywhere. Finally, I gave in and ripped a piece of bread from my sandwich and tossed it over the bird's head.

That was a mistake.

In about a quarter of a millisecond, approximately seven hundred birds from around the globe swooped in on Jamie and me, fluttering around our heads, our chairs, and our food. I couldn't help it. I just screamed and started batting my hands around my head like Fiona Apple, and I was amazed at the power of my own scream until I realized that Jamie was screaming, too. We were covered in birds, dirty, nasty seagulls, and we were still screaming when I heard someone shout to the Lifeguard, "Help! Help! Those old ladies are being eaten by birds!"

"We ARE NOT old!" I screamed as a big fat bird snatched the cookie out of my hand. "We're just Burn Victims dressed like Katherine Hepburn!"

Suddenly, the tide of flapping wings all turned, followed and descended on the bird cookie thief as he fought valiantly to keep his stolen treasure.

"Hey, Granny!" the lifeguard yelled at us, pointing his finger. "Quit feeding those birds!"

"You shut up!" I bellowed back. "I'm a citizen and I have rights! I...I...I lived though the Depression, you know!"

"Oh, what are you talking about?" Jamie said to me. "You had a therapist and a prescription for Celexa!"

"Well, I might just have to go back to that doctor after being mauled by birds," I snipped.

"If you think that was damaging, don't take a gander at what's coming this way," Jamie said in stunned disbelief.

Of course I looked. And there, strutting down the beach was a man with the enormous belly of Santa Claus coming closer, closer, closer, wearing nothing but a Speedo. His belly didn't jiggle with every step; it crashed in waves.

"Oh, God!" I said, wincing as the man came closer. "He has no shame!"

"And not a stitch of pride," Jamie added.

"Blind me! Blind me!" I pleaded to Jamie. "If you care anything about me, squeeze some of that 100 SPF into my eyes, because I cannot take them off of that man!"

"Me, either"! Jamie replied as the man passed directly in front of us.

"Don't just stand there! DO something! STOP HIM!" I yelled to the lifeguard, but he was powerless. He just stood there, his mouth hanging open, in the exact same manner as everyone else on the beach that was hypnotized and frozen by the fat man.

He just looked at all of us and smiled.

"No no no no no no!!!" Jamie gasped in horror as he started to pass us. "No no no no no!"

She was unable to say anything else. In a moment, I learned why. As the fat man passed us, as he glided by with his wicked smile, it was all too apparent. He was not wearing a Speedo.

It was a thong. With a thread of black disappearing up between the hemispheres of his gargantuan, swaying butt. He had done this often, you could tell. There wasn't a tan line on him.

That's a man that knows where to put his sunblock, was all I could say.

ONION HEAD

I looked in the mirror.

And then I screamed.

It was chilling. Terrifying. VIBRANT. It was almost as bad as the time I excused myself to go to the ladies' room halfway through a date, only to discover in my reflection that a subterranean zit had managed to surface like a submarine, and was now flaunting itself as a massive white head in between my eyes, sporting the circumference and illumination of a Tap Light.

Maybe this was worse, I didn't know. All I knew was that I had done something just as bad. As I leaned closer to the mirror to get a better look, I decided that there was no doubt about it.

My hair was purple. Magenta. Fuchsia. Apparently, L'Oreal and I don't share the same opinion of what the word "Cinnamon" means. In fact, I believe that box of hair color should have been named "Eggplant," because the only difference between my head and the vegetable I had in the crisper was that I had lips, since we both share the same chin.

I thought maybe it really wasn't as bad as I thought, perhaps I was being too critical. I was just trying to cover some newly found gray hairs. Was this really worse, I had to ask myself. I found out later that day when I went to pick up my friend Kate and she came to a complete standstill in the middle of the driveway when she saw my purple onion head bobbing around in the driver's seat.

"Hey," she said softly as she got in the car, squinting her eyes.

"You're not going to say anything?" I asked, turning to look at her.

"No, I'm not going to say anything about how your head is the color of the gay Teletubby," she said as she winced. "Can this sun visor move to ninety degrees, because your hair is making my eyes water."

When my husband came home that night, he opened the front door and his face immediately fell.

"Please don't tell me you joined a gang and the next thing you're going to do to is get a tear drop tattoo," he said as he shielded his face with his hand and headed to the bathroom to cry. "My wife is a home girl!"

The next evening when we were having dinner at my Nana's house, my sister was a little more upfront about the hue of my head.

She paused when she saw me, and immediately said, "You look like an old person trying to look young."

I dismissed her comment, since she's pregnant and has the hormones of a lab rat running through her blood.

"Do you like my hair, Nicholas?" I said to my three-year-old nephew.

He paused as well, most likely remembering the "time out" he recently had to serve when he answered my question of, "Do you think Aunt Laurie is fat?"

"Do you like it?" I repeated.

"Well, not exactly," he said, avoiding my eyes. "It's very purple. Are you pretending to be Barney? Barney's only a little bit fat."

"Why are you dyeing your hair, anyway?" my sister prodded. "Don't you remember what happened the last time you did that?"

Indeed, I did, there was no way I could forget. Several years ago, after I felt the compelling urge to become a spunky redhead, I woke up one morning and to find that my head had doubled in size, though that wasn't due to my newly improved self-esteem as a "River Dancin' firecracker." It was mostly due to the allergy my skin had developed toward hair color of any shade. Of any permanence. Of any type at all. With my frizzy red hair and my puckered, bulging face, my mother threw me in the car, headed toward the emergency room and screamed, "You're that big-headed boy in *Mask!* That's what you get for trying to deny your heritage!!"

My face continued to grow, eerily equaling the proportions of Rosie O'Donnell's, though little did I know then that after I quit smoking later that year and gained the required 30 pounds, those proportions would become permanent.

After the allergy was diagnosed in the emergency room, I had to pull down my pants and get a big, long shot in my right cheek while my mom watched. It was sick and it made me feel dirty.

"I hope you heard what that doctor said!" she lectured me on the way home as I held my glasses in front of my face because they would no longer fit across the jack o'lantern it had become. "It's like being allergic to bees or peanut butter! Hair dye can kill! It's like heroin! Do you want me to have to tell my friends that you died of a Miss Clairol overdose? Do you? *Do you?"*

My sister didn't need to remind me of that, because even though I had taken a double dose of Claritin and was very careful about not getting any hair dye on my scalp this time, I could already feel that the purple onion was staring to get rather soggy and engorged with fluid, just like if you poured Italian dressing over it. When I got home, I downed another dose of Claritin, lit a candle and prayed that God would not see fit to take me into the hereafter with gang girl hair. I stayed awake for as long as I could manage. I was afraid that if I went to sleep I would never recover from the deep purple coma, would have to live in a crib in my mother's extra bedroom and she would see my butt on a fairly regular basis.

The next morning, I awoke from a fitful sleep, a nightmare in which I lying in my crib, was wearing an adult-sized onesie, consuming liquefied chicken cutlets and lentil soup intravenously and hearing my mother scream at me, "I said one wink for number one and two winks for number two! Even a real eggplant could figure that out!"

I woke up, opened my eyes and touched my head. The swelling had been reduced. I thanked God.

I kept thanking God fifteen minutes later as I stood in the ABCO check out line with a box in my hand, praying to the Almighty that L'Oreal and I shared the same opinion of what "Dirt" looked like.

And hoping that tomorrow, if I woke up, it wouldn't be as a giant russet potato.

Dear Netflix: Please stop recommending movies I will like because I gave "Legally Blonde" four stars. That was not me, but someone else who lives in my house and watched it when I was not home to mock him.

THE RETURNED

By the look on the faces of the other people standing in line, I should have known then to cut my losses and just abandon my mission altogether.

All I had to do was return a can of wood stain at the home improvement store, an easy enough task. But as soon as I glanced to the first of two return counters, the possibility became real that getting four dollars and sixty-four cents back might take me quite a while.

There, on the counter, were clods of dirt as big as a fist, scattered recklessly as the customer they belonged to pointed a craggy, crooked finger at the cashier. "You sold me bad petunias!" she accused. "And I want my money back!"

Now, the way I perceive the process of returning something to a store is that it's a version of a tiny Lilliputian trial, and from the movies I've seen on cable TV, it's exactly like the legal system in Thailand. Someone calls your number, you produce evidence, are at the mercy of a grumpy, poorly dressed, and in some cases, a hung-over low-wage employee who waves their little piece of power like it was a scepter. You are the plaintiff, the defective object is the defendant, and the cashier is the judge. Your receipt, by the way, is your whole case. It's clear and convincing evidence and frankly, it's the only hope you've got. When it comes to the return line, your friend Marge's eye witness account that the faulty petunias were indeed purchased at this store will do you about as much good as Mark Fuhrman's testimony, so without that receipt, not even a collect call to 1-800-THE-WOLF can help you.

So naturally, the woman attempting to return the petunias, which were now merely big round balls of dirt, had no such receipt. No such proof. The cashier looked at her with disdain, for the woman's case was essentially as dead as the flowers and she knew it.

"I'm sorry, dirt balls can't be exchanged for flowers," she explained.

Instead of accepting her fate and swallowing the $1.67 she claimed the home improvement store owed her in The Swindle of the Rotten Petunias, the woman resorted to her only option, which I understood all too well. You see, when your looks have receded, much like your gums, and the only thing your charm can get you is a free well drink from a lonely, desperate pudgy man in an airport bar, you have no other choice but to engage in hostility and aggression to get your way. It's sad, but it's true, and personally, I can't wait for the day when Britney Spears learns that lesson for herself.

In any case, the woman's move was entirely predictable, any of the people waiting in the return line could have called it.

"If you won't give my my money back," the petunia killer said, "Then I want to see your manager!"

By this time, the woman had sucked 15 minutes of life from everyone waiting in line, so I did not feel the least bit bad when I fake gasped and muttered to the man next to me, "Oh no, not the manager! The Petunia Killer is going for an appeal at the Supreme Court of Returns!"

He man next to me giggled, and so did the lady next to him.

"I mean, if I pulled up all of the clumps of dirt from dead plants in my yard and returned them, I could walk right out of here and landscape The White House!"

A couple of other people laughed, and that's when I realized I had an audience. And for all intensive purposes, they were captive!

"I'm going to start bringing in every twig I find in the street if she pulls this off," I quipped, and was rewarded with a round of hearty chuckles.

"One Rose Garden, coming up!" I smarmily commented, which was met with peals of laughter.

"I mean, how do you kill a petunia, anyway?" I chortled, now obviously on a roll. "It's not like it's an orchid. The petunia is clearly the whore in the annual world."

My audience just looked at me in silence.

"That wasn't very funny," the man next to me whispered.

But the Petunia Killer was not done. When the manager arrived, she did offer proof in the form of a torn, dirty plastic six-pack container that she pulled from her other bag as more clods of dirt tumbled out.

Frankly, when I plant something, I like to have a little hope, and part of that optimism is tossing the black plastic six-pack it came in. I free it to my recycling bin, the first stop in a journey that will result in it floating in an ocean far, far away from me, poisoning the wildlife on a continent I will probably never visit.

That kind of hope is necessary in gardening.

Hanging onto the container just screams that you aren't going to give it your all; that you might sprinkle some Miracle Gro, the blue crystal meth of the planting world around and hope for the best. In fact, it seems a little premeditated if you ask me.

Do you know what it takes to kill a petunia? Like I said, the petunia is the crack whore of flowering species, and I do, by the way, happen to think that is pretty goddamn funny. But you really have to try to kill one. You have to forget to water it for basically a season. You have to put it in a closet and deny the sun even exists for creatures like that. And to produce the balls of dirt that were now crumbling on the returns counter, you had to be merciless. Have no conscience. Have no guilt.

You had to be a psychopath.

"Fine," the manager said as the woman shook a clod at him and sprayed bits of dried-up earth around like confetti. "I'll make an exchange. Go back to Garden and get another one."

The witnesses, including myself, gasped.

She had done it. Gotten away with it.

Scott free.

"Wait a minute," I said, standing up, presenting my tiny can of wrong color stain.

The line grew quiet.

"In my hands," I began. "I have a can of stain that I need a refund for, three times the investment you made in those petunias."

The line looked at me. I threw up my other hand.

"And I have the receipt."

People audibly gasped.

"And I will give them to you, Petunia Lady," I said as I started walking over to her and she reached out her hands. "Cash refund."

"Under one condition," I said, stopping short two feet from her.

She looked at me.

"You must give an allocution," I said simply.

The oldest lady waiting in the return line covered her mouth and whispered, "A Jack McCoy move!"

"What?" the Petunia Killer said.

"*Confess,*" I said clearly. "And promise that you will never go near petunias again."

"And I get the whole amount?" she said.

"Sing it, sister," I replied.

"I forgot to water them," she said matter of factly. "For a day."

I shook my head and pulled the receipt away.

"For two days."

I shook my head.

"For a week?"

I started at her.

"OK, ever. I never even planted them. It was too hot."

"They died in that six-pack, didn't they?" I asked, casting a glance at the people in the return line.

She looked down at the floor. "Yes," she remitted. "On my patio."

"At least you didn't leave them in the car," I said, shaking my head in shame.

She looked away.

"Then I'm adding another condition," I said. "Stay away from annuals!! And perennials!! Who knows how much spilled chlorophyll you have on your hands!"

"Fine," she said, reaching for the receipt.

I snatched it away. "From now on, you are only allowed to buy cactus and the very ugliest of succulents. Understood?"

She nodded briefly and I turned over the goods. She placed them on the counter and the manager sprung the cash register open, and delivered her her $4.64.

I watched as she took her winnings and went to her car, got in and drove away. The petunias were safe. For now.

Then I went back inside to the paint department, and bought the smallest can of what I thought was most likely going to be a wrong color of stain.

Overheard at breakfast today, said by a 70-year old woman in a tightly curled wig and wearing a Raiders jersey: "It's all about where you keep it. I put it right where I can reach it, so if I let someone in the car I can get my gun right away if things turn funny."

SUING THE MAN

"I was wondering," my husband said into the phone after he called me at work, "Would you happen to know anything about a cardboard box on the front porch the size of a coffin?"

"Hmmmm," I replied. "By my calculations, it's our new coffee table. Or it could be an albino tiger. Or a canoe."

"I see," my husband replied. "So might you also know why there's a back hoe trying to push through our back gate?"

"Oh," I replied. "Those are the pool guys."

"We don't have a pool," my husband said.

"We will tomorrow," I answered.

"So then, can you tell me who the guy is on our roof with a tape measure and an ax?" my husband continued.

"Oh, that would be the contractor," I added. "We're building a second story so I can have my own bedroom!"

"And then who is the lady in our bathroom dressed like a cocktail waitress?" he wanted to know,

"And that would be the maid," I answered smugly. "She's going to have her own room, too."

"Did you, by any chance, sell a body part?" my husband slowly asked. "Or a kilo of cocaine? Or babies over the Internet? How are you paying for this?"

"You should have asked that question when I said albino tiger," I exclaimed. "I got a letter from my lawyer today and baby, we're going to be rich!"

"You don't have a lawyer," he injected.

"I didn't until I opened the mailbox," I answered. "But honey, we're suing THE MAN!"

Finally, after years of believing in karma and subscribing to the theory that what goes around comes around, I had actually seen it happen, more precisely on a lawyer's letterhead. And frankly, I had waited nearly all of my lifetime to read what that letter said.

It said that the bank who had issued my credit card was mean.

It said that the bank who issued my credit card cheated, lied and stole from people.

And that the bank who issued my credit card had not only been mean, but they had also cheated, lied and stolen FROM ME under the guise of fake late fees.

I fell to my knees.

"I'm a VICTIM!" I cried out, my arms stretched up toward heaven. "I'm a VICTIM! I always knew it, I could always feel it, I just didn't know whose victim I was! Thank you, who ever you are, thank you! Now, I feel WHOLE!"

And the story just gets better. Not only was I preyed upon, but I was about to conduct some major Rambo revenge on a corporate giant, since I was included as a plaintiff against my bank in the lawsuit. I WAS FIGHTING BACK against corporate America! I felt just like Michael Moore! All I needed to do was find a guy named Roger!

I mean, this was a dream come true. All of those years, through all of the pain that bank caused me, always calling me up in the middle of the day to ask why my payment was late, when was I going to pay it and how much? And adding all of the late fees and over limit fees, some of which it turned out had a slim chance of not even being real! Gimme, gimme, gimme! In fact, the bank called me more than any of my boyfriends did.

"You know," I had to tell one credit card person years ago who was stalking me and my checkbook, "you should really think about this. If you really want your money, adding 25 dollars to my bill is bad strategy. See, it's just another 25 bucks you're never going to get out of this deadbeat. I'm sorry to say it, but you're reading more into this relationship than what's really there. You're leading yourself on." Then that bank would send me notices and bills all the time, some stamped with a very embarrassing "URGENT: FINAL NOTICE" in red ink on the front! I mean, my mailman *sees* those!

So finally, it was my turn to say, "Hey, bank! Yeah, you!!! You wanna piece of me? Well, come and take a big bite of lawsuit pie, bubba!"

Now I had revenge, and soon I was going to get money. Lawsuit money, more money than I even thought I'd get by slamming on my breaks when driving in front of a Mercedes! More money than starting my own church! More money than throwing myself down a flight of stairs at work! It's true, I said as I pinched myself, this is better than my dreams of collecting disability!

And then, the lawsuit was settled, I got the check, and I realized that the bank was no longer going to be the only one for calling me for their money. I guess the bank must have gypped a lot of people, like the population of China, because my share wasn't going to buy me a second story, a pool, or even a coffee table.

My award, in round numbers, was an even 31 cents. I'd have to get 100 other plaintiffs to chip in to even celebrate with champagne. However, now when the contractor, the pool people, the albino tiger breeder and maid call and demand their money, all I have to say is, "Back off, buddy, or I'll sue you! I've done it before, you know!"

But you know, I still have hope. In other words, if you look up and see me through your peace sign hood ornament, I'd change lanes if I were you.

TAG TEAMED

"If you do not eat that cheese crisp," I said, shaking my finger at my four-year old nephew, "We ARE NOT going to get ice cream, see a movie or go to Disneyland Europe when Mommy comes home!"

In a little less than the 45 minutes since my sister left me in the care of her two sons, ages four and one, the unthinkable had happened. I was just supposed to be the babysitter for a couple of hours while my sister and her husband attended a work-related function. It was supposed to be as simple as that. An adult watching two kids. We would play. We would eat dinner. And then, the kids would go to bed and I would eat all of the ice cream in the freezer. My sister buys the expensive kind. That was the plan.

To tell the truth, the only people I really had experience in babysitting in the past ten years, however, were very drunk dates. There were some similarities between them and infants, I thought to myself. Kids fall asleep in a sitting position, drool consistently, throw up on themselves and others, always need to be held up, make absolutely no sense when they speak and wet themselves while clothed. Clearly, I had the upper hand.

But I should have known something was up when I got to my sister's house at the designated time and she had written out two pages of instructions *per child* about what they could eat, what they could watch on TV and the things we were allowed to do without the potential for getting the police or paramedics involved.

"Do I need to memorize this before you leave?" I asked in a panic.

"Well, not all of it," she replied wincing. "Just the part about open flame, standing buckets of water, and leaving the keys in the ignition of a running car."

"Oh, God," I said, reaching for a pen to write the reminders on my hand.

She wasn't even out of the driveway before things started to fall apart.

"Grandma bought me a vet's kit," Nicholas, the four-year-old said. "Do you want to play, Aunt Laurie?"

"Well, I don't know," I said honestly. "What's in that kit? Flashbacks, a grenade, Agent Orange?"

"It's to make sick animals better," he explained, bringing out a bunch of little plastic medical tools. "Now let me check your heart. And your reflexes. Okay, now lay down on your belly."

"Are you checking my hooves now?" I asked

"No, I'm taking your temperature," he said as he pulled out a toy thermometer. "And this goes up your bum."

I couldn't have shot up faster if a bolt of lightening had hit me.

"You are so NOT putting that thing up my butt," I said sharply, backing up. "I don't care what you've heard, but Aunt Laurie doesn't play games like that. I am not that kind of...cow. Hey! Keep your hands where I can see them!"

"I'm hungry for a cheese crisp," Nicholas said, and then pointed toward his brother's bedroom. "And I think David is waking up."

I got the baby and put him in the high chair, made a cheese crisp according to my sister's two-page directions and opened a jar of applesauce for David. When I came at him with a spoon, he suddenly became defensive, his pudgy arms taking on the proportions of a pin-ball flipper and knocking the spoon out of my hand.

"I hate my cheese crisp," Nicholas said.

"Eat the cheese crisp!" I said, going in for another try with the spoon, which this time hit me on the cheek. "...Or I'm taking back all the toys I bought for you that are in my car *right now*."

"Then I don't want to wear pants," Nicholas replied, taking off his clothes while another round of applesauce was coming my way. "Winnie the Pooh doesn't wear pants, and neither do I."

"And that bear should be arrested!" I retorted, amazed at the pain applesauce can cause when it smacks your retina at 30 miles per hour. "You'd think that if the idiot was only capable of dressing half of himself, someone over at Disney would figure out which half it was important to cover up! Now get dressed and eat the cheese crisp!"

"Humbee woombee wa-wa!" Nicholas said as he shrugged at me and threw up his arms.

"Oh no!" I said, struggling to get the next spoonful somewhere near Flipper Boy's face. "Don't you talk to me in that secret language! I'm telling you right now that you'd better eat that cheese crisp or...."

I paused for a moment, and remembered my mother's secret weapon when she needed to badly retain control, and then I got ready to use it.

"...OR I'm sending you to the ORPHANAGE!!!!"

There. I had done it. Ha ha! I didn't want to, but I had to show him who the boss was. I showed him! I was waiting for him to cave in when all of a sudden, it hit me:

It had taken 45 minutes and two children to turn me into my mother.

Nicholas looked at me. "Did you really mean that, Aunt Laurie?" he asked.

Then I was shamed. Shamed by a pantless, four-year old secret language talker who had tried to assault me with a thermometer. This is what you get, I told myself, for coming over just to eat free ice cream. I was pathetic.

"I didn't mean it," I said, avoiding eye contact. "And I'm sorry I said that. I was wrong."

"I don't want to go to an orphanage!" Nicholas said, then burst out crying.

"No, no, no," I pleaded, trying to calm him down. "I don't even know where one is close by! I'd probably have to take you to Romania, and I don't have enough miles. As it is, I need to fly to New York before I can earn enough to get an upgrade for my flight to LA."

He stopped heaving his little lungs up and down and composed himself. "What's an orphanage?"

"Oh, you know," I said, not knowing what what going to come out of my mouth in the next second. "It's a place where kids with no parents sleep in the same crib and then roam around in diapers and no one really watches them and the TV is on all day."

"I want to go to an orphanage," he said immediately. "Can we go now?"

Oh God. I sighed.

"I have a better idea," I said, swallowing my dignity. "How about you take my temperature? And then eat all of Mommy's ice cream?"

"By the way," I felt compelled to say to the guy at the drive-thru window as I paid for my Taco Supreme, "Am I the only one who has mentioned that the picture on the menu of the new Biscuit Taco looks largely like a spread in Hustler?"

The Good Deed

She had blue hair and thick glasses in black frames.

Of medium height and somewhat chubby, she approached me hesitantly as my friend Jamie and I waited in the will call line.

With frizzy, curly locks and a pronounced double chin, the girl looked just like me.

I've heard of this thing before; people who could be twins suddenly running into each other when they least expected it. For a moment I froze as various scenarios ran through my head:

SCENARIO ONE: A look-alike stalker from Phoenix has followed me to Los Angeles and is now going to shoot me as I wait to pick up tickets for the 10:30 p.m. performance of "Kids in the Hall";

SCENARIO TWO: Then she stabs me.

SCENARIO THREE: She thinks I am Janeane Garafalo, will ask for an autograph and will be severely disappointed when I give her one.

SCENARIO FOUR: We are both the love twins from an illicit rendezvous between Sophia Loren and either Paul Newman, David Niven or Peter Ustinov during the filming of "Lady L" in 1965, only to be separated at birth and given to nice Italian families in the Brooklyn/Queens area. I have suspected this for quite some time, although I never had any proof before now, since my mother always refused to answer any questions about the subject. "You live in a fantasy world," she always said. "I want you to tell your doctor about this one. I have a fantasy, too. you know. It's called 'That Hairy Daughter of Mine Picks Up a Razor and Shaves Her Damn Legs!'"

The girl came closer.

"Hi," she said as she nervously waved her hand.

"Please don't shoot or stab me," I said quickly. "I'm Janeane Garafalo and I'm happy to sign your hand, but if we're sisters, we should probably just hug and then call Sally Jesse Raphael."

She just looked at me. "I was wondering if you could do me a favor," she said, backing up a bit.

"Absolutely. I will TOTALLY do DNA testing," I assured her. "I'm hoping it was David Niven, aren't you? He had a great accent. Peter Usitinov would explain my inability to diet, and I would be so disappointed if Paul cheated on Joanne, wouldn't you?"

"Sure," she said after a long pause. "But I just wanted to know if you would help me. See, I was at the first show and I wanted to buy a poster afterward, but they ushered us out of there so fast that I couldn't get back to the lobby. So I was wondering if, when you went in, if I gave you the money, you could get that poster and give it to me though the door."

"Oh," I said to my almost sister. "Oh no. I don't think so."

"Please?" she asked, cupping her hands together. "It would mean so much to me!"

"Um," I said as I thought about it, "No."

"Oh, *please*," she begged.

To me, it just sounded like one big hassle, and I wouldn't even do that for a real sister, let alone a stranger posing as one. Suddenly, I started hearing my seventh-grade self in my head.

"That girl is going to get you in trouble!" the voice said. "Get you all mixed up with a bad crowd, try to take you for a ride in a Camaro! Don't take any gum from her, it probably has LSD on it!"

As soon as I remembered that *I* was the kid in the bad crowd and that no self-serving dope addict would ever waste drugs on a stranger, I realized the warning was not in my voice but my mom's and I relaxed a bit.

I looked at the blue girl. "Hang on a second," I said to her as I pulled Jamie aside.

"We are NOT buying her a poster," Jamie said immediately. "These tickets were expensive, I've waited forever for this show and I'm not going to get thrown out by trying to smuggle contraband for a Little Girl Blue over there!"

"I know, I know," I agreed. "But this is what I'm thinking. We're miserable people, right?"

"Well, yeah," Jamie agreed. "And selfish and mean."

"Yes," I agreed. "But what if we were to do a good deed? Maybe if we did something good, I'm thinking that we'd get something good back in return."

"Like we could claim eight dependents on our taxes and not get caught?" Jamie asked. "Or maybe a bank teller could get our bank accounts mixed up with a charity's and make us rich?"

I nodded.

"Fork over the cash," Jamie yelled to the blue girl as we headed into the theater. "We're in business."

So we bought the poster, even gave the blue girl her correct change back, minus ten bucks for our troubles, and headed up toward our seats. We were sitting there for approximately 30 seconds when a man with a head the size of a pumpkin sat in front of me, and his melon-headed wife sat in front of Jamie.

"I can't see anything!" Jamie hissed. "The good deed is NOT paying off!"

"Don't worry," I assured her. "It's probably on it's way up there, but it hasn't been approved, stamped or filed yet. Give it some time. Maybe halfway through they'll get violently ill and have to leave."

The show started, and even though we couldn't see anything, we could still catch some jokes by listening very hard. That lasted three minutes until a girl with a horse laugh sat directly behind us and began hee-hawing very loudly every time someone on stage said something. Said anything.

"This sucks," Jamie said. "I'm never doing anything nice again!"

When we heard people clapping and realized the show was over, we headed out with everyone else.

"I think I want a T-shirt," Jamie said in a solemn voice. "Since we didn't see the show, I might as well have something to remember this by."

As we tromped down the stairs, however, an usher was directed everyone out an emergency exit door which opened onto the alley.

"HEY!" Jamie yelled. "That's not fair! I need to get to the lobby to get a T-shirt!"

"I don't care," the usher said as he pointed us to the door.

"But I want a T-shirt!" Jamie relented as we entered the alley. "I DESERVE a T-shirt!"

From the darkened shadows, a little voice popped up.

"Did someone say they wanted a T-shirt?" the voice said as a Kids in the Hall T-shirt danced in front of Jamie, taunting her. "I have a poster, too...."

"How much?" Jamie asked.

"Cost plus 20 bucks," the voice said, stepping into the light.

Jamie and I just looked at each other.

"Good deeds never go unrewarded," the blue girl said. "Consider it a family discount."

Ok, so here is my solution to the excessively long lines to the ladies' restroom during theater intermission:

ESTABLISH A FART CORRAL.

This way every old lady who only has to blast a GI bomb simply goes to the Fart Corral to release. Based on my experience last night, this would cut the line down by 95%, and those people who drank way too much wine at dinner actually have the opportunity to urinate. Because at half time, it was like an ass symphony down there. Oboes, trumpets, tubas. Not one flute. And barely a tinkle. Also, if you are 75 years old and you blow a Louie Armstrong next to me, you have lived long enough to learn to flush the toilet at the same time. Seriously.

WALTER

I guess I would be lying if I said that Walter doesn't scare me.

Sometimes when I'm alone in the house and I hear a floorboard creak or something drop in the kitchen, I'll admit that a silver shiver runs up my spine much like it does when my mother says she's planning on dropping by my house. The difference is that I know that upon setting foot past the threshold, Walter doesn't scan my baseboards and comment that there's enough dog hair down there to fill a comforter or ask, "How much did you say you paid for this house again?" followed closely by, "Boy, did you get robbed...."

But Walter does things that my mother would never even consider. For instance, he has a full stable of tricks, including locking my husband in his office, turning on the radio at full blast at 3:15 in the morning and setting off the burglar alarm minutes after we've fallen back asleep. My mom would never do that. The craziest thing she's ever done was drink two margaritas and then try to tell me a dirty joke, which was enough to keep me in therapy for another year.

But Walter can get away with these things because there are no consequences for him. Because Walter, you see, is a ghost.

Now, to tell the truth, I didn't really know that Walter existed until my friend Gertie, a practicing psychic, told me so. She held my hand one day and told me that something was about to happen to my kidneys and that I had a ghost attached to me. Soon after, the radio was going off in the middle of the night and two weeks later, I was in the emergency room with kidney stones.

And I had someone to blame for the eleven extra pounds I had suddenly and inexplicably gained.

Now, I have to admit, there is something overtly sexy about having your own ghost. My friends can boast about their children taking their first steps, or forming their first sentence and all I have to do is yawn and respond, "Yes, but can they pass through solid objects and transcend all time and space like my Walter?" Hands down, that one's mine. I mean, how many people have their own ghost? It's like I'm living a sixties' sitcom in my own house, and I'm waiting for Dr. Bombay and my identical, evil cousin Sabrina to pop up on my couch imprisoned in stocks. I even came up with some names for our own show, like "Friends, Even If They're Dead;" "Touched by a Ghost;" "Everyone Loves Laurie and Walter" "I Dream of Walter," and "Be-Waltered." Together on our show, I imagined, Walter and I could play delightful, madcap pranks involving livestock and jungle animals on my nosy neighbor with the Harley and people that send me hate mail all while I wore go-go boots, miniskirts and a wig with a flirty flip.

There are many benefits to having Walter around, especially in the summer. If it gets too hot in the house, all I need to do is summon my goblin and BINGO! I've got a cold spot to sit in, and the best part is that the power company isn't making a dime off of it. Walter has also fulfilled my wildest dreams of having my VERY OWN PERSONAL SCAPEGOAT, which enables my husband to have a lot more free time. Now every time I lose my keys, it's not my responsibility. It's Walter expressing his separation anxiety. When my husband yells that I've left the stove on for for hours or overnight, I can reply with confidence, "No I didn't! Walter must have been hungry!" If we have guests that decide to stay too long, I can always kick over a lamp and say, "Wow, do you feel that energy? Walter's manic phase! We'd better cover the windows with plywood this time!" and before I know it, perpetual guests are asking for their coats.

Of course, there are drawbacks to having Walter around, too. Gertie says Walter loves hats, which was odd, because lately I had been buying a lot of hats, and simply put, that's a tragedy. I have a head the size of a pinto bean, I have no business wearing hats, and now I have more chapeaus than *Columbo*. Then there's Walter's favorite trick--slowly creaking out bedroom door open in the middle of the night. I will agree it is a stunning example in the craft of haunting, it's something you can tell he's spent decades perfecting—but it can be a little chilling, especially if *The Sixth Sense* or the biography of Charles Manson just aired on cable that night.

Now, naturally, my mother doesn't believe in Walter, thinks I'm nuts and keeps saying, "Casper didn't hide your damn keys, you idiot, your brain just has the memory capacity of a hot dog! I'm still waiting to get the Tupperware back that you borrowed from me four years ago! If it's not too much trouble, can you have your phantom friend mail it back to me, please?" And my husband, who despite seeing Walter's work for himself, refuses to believe that my little friend exists and has repeatedly asked me if I'm sure I never got shock treatments.

But it doesn't matter, it really doesn't. Gertie says Walter looks out for me and will most likely hang around forever. I guess I'll never lose those 11 pounds. But that's okay, because even though I know that we'll probably never get NBC interested in the pilot of "Walter Knows Best," as long as there's Walter, I'll get to be Maude.

DO THE THING!!

I was washing dishes when all of a sudden, I thought, "Hey! We should go to the movies!"

I had just turned to yell to my husband in the living room when I saw him standing in the kitchen doorway.

"I just got this idea," he said. "I thought, 'Hey! We should go to the movies!'"

"No way!" I cried. "Because I was thinking *the exact same thing* just now!"

"Wow," my husband said, looking shocked. "That means we did it! We finally did it!"

"Did what?" I asked, getting confused.

"We did the *thing*!" he answered excitedly. "The THING! You know, like a psychic connection! Like we talked to each other in our heads on a level only....soulmates can understand!"

I gasped. "Do you know what that means?" I asked slowly. "It means that we didn't make the biggest mistake of our lives getting married after all! Whew! What a relief!"

"You're telling me!" he agreed. "We're like Yin and Yang!"

"Well, not really," I questioned. "They were joined at the hip and shared a pancreas, honey--I mean, *soulmate!*"

Soulmates. Finally, after five years of marriage, we now had our confirmation. We belonged together! We were made for each other! And because of our telepathic communication, could live an easier life knowing that we would never have to return all of our wedding gifts. We could finally use the can opener and eat on real plates! I mean, sure, I'm pretty positive that we liked each other, but just like any couple, sometimes you just have to stop and say, "Is this guy, who just told me that his dream job is to be the person inside the Godzilla suit who crushes miniature Japanese fishing villages, really the one for me?" or "Is this girl, who got her front teeth lodged into a candy apple and sprained a muscle in her neck by over-aggressively attempting to devour it, really the one for me?" Sometimes, you just have to wonder.

"This makes so much sense now," I had to admit to my husband as we waited in the movie line to buy tickets. "Our destined connection is clearing up so many things for me, like how you're always in the bathroom when I need to use it, you continually eat the last of the leftovers I was planning on having for lunch and you always know the exact thing to say to make me fly into a rage! In hindsight, it's completely amazing!"

"I know! We're like twins!" my husband replied, pinching himself on the arm.

"OUCH!" I chuckled back.

"What should we see?" he asked, looking at the marquis that listed the movies.

"I'm thinking...." I said, putting my fingers to my temples and furrowing my brow.

"Planet of the Apes!" he shouted.

I shook my head in awe. "We are too good," I giggled. "I love the THING!"

When we reached the ticket window, the guy behind the glass somewhat smiled.

"Two for—" my husband said and then pointed at me.

"Planet of the Apes!" I exclaimed.

The ticket guy just stared at us.

"We just did the THING," my husband informed him with a chuckle.

"Great, pal," the guy replied dryly. "But you do the thing in this theater and I'll call the cops. Now, which showing of Planet of the Apes do you want? It's on 21 of our 24 screens."

"The next one," we said at the same, yet unplanned time, I'm sure to the astonishment of all those around us.

Once in the theater, I got the seats while my soul mate went for snacks. Lo and behold, when he returned with the loot, all I could so was shake my head.

"We are so in tune to each other that I'm thinking we should cancel the cell phone because I don't think I need it to track you anymore!" I said, reaching for the chocolate covered raisins that I was indeed craving.

My husband, how ever, pulled back. "Not so fast," he answered. "The raisins are mine. The gummy fish are for you."

"The gummy fish?" I asked, shocked and revolted. "I want the raisins. I hate gummy fish; they'll pull most of my dental work out of my head!"

"Ha, ha, nice try," my husband retorted. "I definitely received a gummy fish message from you when I was waiting in line. Loud and clear: GUMMY FISH FOR SOULMATE. Funny trick!"

"Well, maybe there's a gummy fish junkie honing in to our frequency, but it wasn't me!" I pouted. "Maybe you have another soulmate in this theater."

"Don't be silly," my husband said, popping some raisins in his mouth without offering any to me. "Tune into me now. What am I thinking?"

I tried really hard and closed my eyes for several seconds. "'Coffee makes the skank sleepy,'" I said, repeating the message that popped into my head.

When I opened my eyes, my husband was just staring at me with disbelief. "Not even *close!*" he snapped. "I was recalling the experimental text I'm reading that's centered on a stream of consciousness narrative and yet dabbles with outside stimulus! You're not even *trying!*"

I just shook my head. "Thank God I didn't use the can opener before we left the house," I mentioned. "Read my mind NOW, Brain Boy."

"Sorry, I can't get through with all of that senseless static in your head!" he snapped.

"Oh, I see, I see," I snarled, crossing my arms. "You are so totally sleeping on the couch!"

My husband gasped. "Hooray!" he said. "The THING is back!"

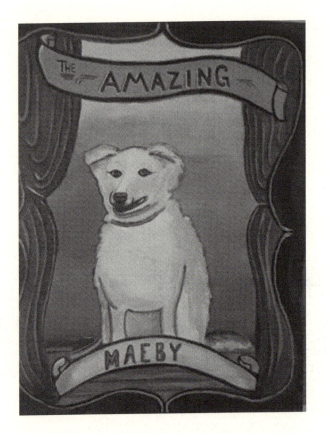

Today, I twice yelled at Maeby very loudly because I thought she was.... deceased in the yard. I felt horrible about it, thinking terrible thoughts and being a freak. Then my husband just came in and said, "I had to yell at Maeby. She was sleeping so deeply, I thought she was dead."

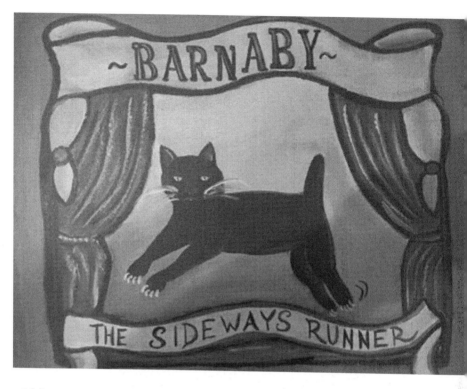

He's been dead for seven years, but his urine lives on and on. And on. Happy Cat Day.

WE'RE STILL HERE

My phone rang last Friday night.

"We're still here...." my cousin Anthony taunted.

"I know, *I know,*" I replied. "I'm sorry that you have 50 gallons of water lining your hallway, I'm sorry that you spent your house payment on Campbell's Chunky soups, I'm sorry you cashed in Amazon.com stock and invested in chemical toilets instead. I'm sorry, *I'm sorry*, I'M SORRY!"

It wasn't the first angry phone call I've received, and I doubt it will be the last. Now several weeks successfully past the Y2K bug, nearly every person I know hasn't hesitated to pick up their receiver, dial my number and harass me.

It's not that I wanted anything to happen at the stroke of midnight on January 1; I didn't want the world to turn into a pumpkin, I didn't want anything to get blown up, but I did want to be ready. Just in case. And I wanted the people I loved to be ready too, because the last thing I planned to do in the year 2000 was open a soup kitchen for hungry friends and relatives who had previously referred to me as "unstable and in need of medication," and my husband as "that poor man."

But as I nervously waited on New Year's Eve, listening to the clock complete 12 chimes, nothing happened. No one was happier than me. Nothing happened, nothing at all, except the phone began to ring.

It started at 12:01 am on January first, as my husband stood out on our front porch looking at the fireworks from downtown, celebrating the fact that nothing had happened and trying very hard not to get shot. Now that we've lived in our neighborhood for several years, we've both become something of acoustic experts.

"It's okay!" my husband shouted as I ran for the door after hearing a loud explosion and he pointed to the sky. "Green sparkler at one o'clock!"

"BANG! BANG! BANG!" I heard again, reaching for the door knob.

"Bottlerocket two streets northwest!" my husband shouted.

"BOOM!" I heard as I covered my head.

"Backfiring Monte Carlo near the park!" he exclaimed.

"Why is the ground shaking?" I cried.

"Bass line of the new Puffy Combs rip-off playing in the Monte Carlo's tape deck," he explained.

"BAM!" I heard. "BAM BAM BAM BAM BAM!!!!"

"Drunken neighbor with an automatic weapon six houses down!" he said as he pushed me to the ground. "DROP!! SEEK COVER!!!"

As soon as we crawled through the door, the phone jingled.

"Hello, Chicken Little," my mother's voice shot when I answered it. "I'm waiting for the sky to fall down, but I think it got caught on the neighbor's satellite dish. Oh wait—yes, the fire department is here, and thank God, they're holding up the sky with their ladders and some very big sticks. And some Scotch tape. You idiot. Do you know what you put us through? Your father almost bought a chemical toilet from your cousin Anthony! I told you nothing was going to happen!"

"Hang on, Mom," I said. "I'm getting another phone call."

"Hey, Nostradamus," my friend Jeff said when I clicked onto the other line. "Do you know what that noise is? It's the TOILET. It's the TOILET FLUSHING. You had my poor pregnant wife scared that she was going to have to poop in a bowl from now on! Here's the sound of the light switch going on and off. You had my poor pregnant wife scared that we were going to have to do our laundry with a rock in the community swimming pool because we wouldn't have electricity!"

"That is *not* what I said," I replied. "I merely suggested that you have some extra water and candles on hand and the address of a midwife. Or a medicine woman educated about primitive birthing conditions. THAT IS ALL I SAID. And I didn't say anything about the pool. I said find a freshwater river or stream! And why are you using the phone, anyway? I told you that could crash the system!"

I clicked over to my mother.

"I have to go," she said quickly. "A tower of canned fruit cocktail just fell on your father."

The phone rang again.

"How are you doing, Doe," my sister said. "Are you wearing your Nike's and a purple sheet? I saw the mothership pass over my house and head your way. Maybe if you make a bonfire with your 600 rolls of toilet paper and use 200 flashlights to line a landing strip you can signal them to stop! Oh, and by the way, Price Club called and they want all of their food back! Hee hee hee! Oh, and China called and they want to know if they can bring India when they come to your house for dinner!! Hee hee hee!"

Just then, the other line beeped.

"Happy New Year!" my friend Meg laughed.

"Thank you," I said wincing, getting ready for the lecture. "I suppose you're angry with me, too."

"Oh, no," Meg answered. "Why would we be mad?"

"Because I told you to buy extra food and water and a generator and you did," I said meekly.

"Oh, we lied about that to shut you up," she said blankly. "Actually, we're thinking about having an intervention for you next week if you don't make an appointment with your doctor. Oh, no! Our lights just went out!"

"Really?" I said excitedly.

"No, I'm lying," Meg laughed again.

I wearily hung up the phone and threw myself on the couch.

"Everyone hates me," I whined to my husband. "My friends, my family. I just wanted the people I loved to be ready! Was that so wrong? Now Meg wants to have an intervention!"

My husband nervously put his hands in his pockets and looked around.

"What do you know about this?" I asked him as I sat up.

"Nothing, nothing," he assured me. "Nothing. I just said we could have it here."

"Fine," I agreed. "We can have it here. There's more than enough Dinty Moore Beef Stew for everyone. And everyone gets a can of fruit cocktail every time they say they're worried about me. At least then I can reach some of my shoes again."

HIDEOUS

"DAD! DAD! DAD!" the four-year old boy in the row ahead of me yelled. "WHY ARE WE STOPPING, DAD? WHY ARE WE TURNING AROUND, DAD? AREN'T WE TAKING OFF, DAD?"

I dug my nails into the backs of my hands to keep from screaming. The plane my husband, our friend Duane and I had boarded to take us back to Phoenix from our vacation in Michigan had been headed toward the runway when all of a sudden, it came to a complete halt and then taxied right back to the gate.

The child in the row ahead and to the left of us had not stopped talking since we got on the plane a half an hour before. I could not see him; I could only see his father, dressed in sweatpants and tight T-shirt with yellow armpit stains, who was seated in the aisle seat, directly adjacent to me.

"DAD, WHEN ARE WE GOING, DAD? ARE WE STILL GOING TO LEGOLAND, DAD?" the kid bellowed. "CAN I HAVE ANOTHER SODA, DAD? HUH, HUH, CAN I, DAD? CAN I?"

The father turned and nodded slowly, then turned back around, just as the pilot announced over the intercom that the generator was off-line and needed to be repaired before we were going anywhere. That was the signal for everyone to get up, go to the bathroom, and, naturally, recline their seats all the way back.

Personally, I think reclining needs to be outlawed, because what the passenger in front of you takes for himself he takes away from YOU. You have paid for that space. I believe seats should be fully equipped with an "Guess again, La-Z-Boy!!" button on the back side of every headrest to automatically shoot these space suckers back into the upright position.

I know my husband would second this. In front of him, a man the size of circus peanut pushed his seat smack into the lap of my 6'2" husband, who gasped in pain as the peanut man's head pummeled and then essentially rested on our family jewels.

"DAD! DAD!" the child in front of us wailed. "WE'VE BEEN HERE FOR THREE HOURS, DAD! ARE WE GOING TO LIVE HERE FOREVER AND EVER, DAD? I FINISHED MY SODA, DAD! CAN I HAVE MORE, DAD?"

I leaned forward, cradled my head in my hands and quietly beat my skull against the seat in front of me. The kid was right. By that time, we had been on the plane for three hours.

"Honey," my husband gasped as he tried to reach out to me over the peanut head. "It's going to be OK, just don't be alarmed when I finally stand up and it looks like I've got a couple of eggplants in my pants."

"DAD! DAD!" the kid shouted. "I HAVE TO GO TO THE BATHROOM, DAD. CAN I BRING MY SOCK PUPPET, DAD? CAN I? GUESS WHAT RHYMES WITH BUDDY, DAD? BUDDY! BUDDY AND BUDDY! THAT RHYMES, DAD! BUDDY AND BUDDY!"

The dad got up and stood in the aisle, waiting for his progeny. When the child scooted out and finally appeared, my husband gasped.

The boy looked just like Sergeant Carter in *Gomer Pyle*, complete with crew-cut, beer gut and big, brown dime-sized freckles. His head was as big as any man's, and his plump skin puckered at joints and glowed a pasty Detroit white.

"It's... *hideous*!" my husband shrieked.

"WANNA SEE WHAT AN AIRPLANE BATHROOM LOOKS LIKE, SOCK DOG?" the boy bellowed to the spongy sock puppet that was barking on his hand. "ARF! ARF! I THOUGHT SO, SOCK DOG!"

"It's times like this that make me wish I had never stopped doing drugs!" I said between poundings. "Everything was so quiet then! There was no noise! Just a buzz! And some colors! I can't handle all of this humanity!"

"Is this plane going to be fixed when the pilot takes off?" an older woman asked a passing flight attendant as she chomped like a horse on the rind of a bagel. "Because I don't want to fly on a broken plane, you know! I paid full fare!"

"It's not like the pilot is on the ground commandeering the plane from a remote control joystick!" I yelled to my purple husband, loud enough for the elderly woman to hear. "He's *on* it!"

"Good news!" the pilot announced. "The generator is back online; we should be off the ground in a matter of minutes!"

A round of cheers went up.

"SOCK DOG WANTED TO DRINK OUT OF THE POTTY, DAD!" The Sergeant Carter child said as he stomped back down the aisle. "IT WASN'T MY FAULT, DAD! IT WASN'T, DAD!"

I pulled on the dad's sweatpants as he passed by. "I have four TheraFlu Nighttime capsules in my purse," I said imploringly as I looked into his eyes. "And I will give you 50 dollars if you feed them to your kid."

"Passengers, we have a slight problem," the pilot said over the intercom again. "We have what appears to be a large blockage in the SkyPort toilet and we won't be going anywhere until the problem is fixed."

I looked at the kid's hand. It was freckled and empty.

"Deal's off," I said letting go of the sweatpants. "I think I'm ready to see some colors."

I, for one, would really like Madonna and Sean Penn to get back together again. I'd like to think they've both matured and that now after a fight, Sean would not tie her to a chair in a closet but just cancel her Botox appointments.

WILL AND TESTAMENT

I had a nightmare.

I was on an airplane to San Francisco, had been passed by when the flight attendant was handing out pretzels (apparently my dream was a Peanut-Free Zone). I was about to complain when the plane took a nose dive and the lights went out. I was about to die, and suddenly, I became very scared. I realized my mom was going to bury what was left of me in my prom dress, and if I had any hair, I knew she was going to put it in hot rollers.

I woke with a horrified start. I looked at the clock, it was 2:14 a.m. and I had to catch a plane in four hours. I realized that even if I came to my mother in spirit form before the funeral, she would look at my ghost, put her hands on her hips and say, "If you think I'm going to bury you in those damn overalls, you're not only out of your body, you're out of your mind. Is that *really* what you plan on wearing for all of eternity? You look like Eddie Albert in *Green Acres*. Don't you *dare* meet the Virgin Mary looking like that! She'll think you're the maid! Would it kill you to put on a dress and some hose for the afterlife? WOULD IT?!"

Thoughts started racing through my head about all the chaos my death would cause. Within days, I'm sure my husband would be found, barefoot and wandering the streets in a T-shirt and his boxers, asking strangers and fearful neighbors, "Have you seen my socks? Have you seen the can opener? I don't know where she kept the milk! I can't find anything! If you were a fork, where would you be? WHERE WOULD YOU BE???"

I had my loved ones to think about.

At 2:16, I hoped out of bed and ran to my office. I had to do it, otherwise horrible things were going to happen. I could not trust my husband to properly dispose of my mortal remains, either, because he keeps insisting that when he "expires," I'm to lay his body outside and let birds eat him or bury him in the desert under some stupid tree. Once, I came home and found him dressed in a green and red poncho, so I know he's not kidding.

I started typing.

MY WILL

Hi everybody, I guess I'm dead.

Thanks for gathering here today. I would have rather left a video tape, but as you've all pointed out, I've put on a few "happy pounds" and would rather not have the last image of me be confused with Monica Lewinsky's testimonial tape for Jenny Craig.

For my burial, you'd better put me someplace where there's air conditioning. I don't want to be dead *and* hot. You can cremate me if funds are tight, I don't care, parts is parts, but my final resting place must be equipped with climate control and preferably a fan for some white noise so I can sleep at night.

Don't let mom dress me. This is very important. The last thing I need is to try and make a new afterlife for myself dressed in black taffeta, a pink sash and a hoop skirt, unless I meet a cute Civil War veteran, which is unlikely, since proper dental hygiene only became common place in the last century.

I request that the Funeral Banquet is composed of spray cheese, Chocolate Twizzlers and Yoo-Hoos. Afterward, everyone can gather around and reminisce about how I enriched all of your lives, but NO ONE is allowed to tell the story about the time I drank a fifth of Jack Daniels, passed out on the potty and woke up the next morning with my panties around my ankles and the dog helping himself to the throw up on the shower walls.

Okay, now for my earthly belongings.

Mom, you get all the stuff you bought from QVC and subsequently unloaded on me. That includes the food dehydrator, the food moisturizer, the manual treadmill that was so hard to use I burst a vein in my eye and the spray-on hair for my bald spot, I mean "cow lick."

To my sister Lisa, who believes the Y2K problem is a rumor spread by Hormel, manufacturers of potted meat, I bequeath 18 jars of Skippy Reduced-Fat Crunchy Peanut Butter and 24 cans of tuna from my own personal stockpile. You'll find them in my clothes closet under the purifier that turns urine into water. You can also have the little packets of mayonnaise I've been pocketing from Schlotsky's so you can make a nice little sandwich when the world explodes. I also leave you a package of unopened maxi pads and 18 Tampax you'll find in the bathroom closet behind the beef jerky and a six-pack of creamed canned corn.

To my other sister, user name BeanieQueenie, I give to you my collection of *Little House on the Prairie* artifacts, including the ice skates without the blades that I made into pioneer boots and the sunbonnet I made from construction paper. I leave you these because in 1976, you insisted we watch Monday Night Football the same night the blind school burned down and Mom said it was your turn. You won. Open those *Little House* books, Beanie, and may you come to love Pa, Mary and Laura the way I have. THEN you'll know the pain you caused by not letting me see the blind school smolder!

To Dad, I leave you the car that I only paid you back $125 for. Word to the wise; Before you move it, renew the insurance because I kind of let it lapse last year.

Nothing in my house is clean enough to leave to Nana.

To my husband, my wonderful, patient, sweet husband, I leave you my memory and the knowledge that because of you, I became a better person. Should the idea of remarrying ever cross your mind, rest assured that I'll will come back quicker than a fart and scare you until you wet the bed when that slut is laying on my side. If you're lonely, call my mother!

Good night, sweet princess! (Oh, that's me!)

XOXO, Laurie

With my will complete, I boarded the plane with peace in my heart, confident that I had taken care of my family.

It wasn't until the flight attendant forgot to give me my pretzel pack that I realized I forgot to tell my husband where his socks were.

He'll never find them, although they're right where they should be, in his second dresser drawer, under the five-pound sack of powdered eggs and ham.

Nothing like getting a surprise package in the mail, tearing it open and discovering it's a toddler dish from a pharmaceutical company that tells you, "Hey, Fatty! The salad goes in the big part, the potatoes in the small part. And no, there is no compartment for dessert. Did I mention that you're fat?"

Dear Readers:

This probably concludes the series of Vintage Legends, unless another crop of forgotten pieces pops up, which is always possible. Thank you so much for supporting my writing, for reading, and for making me laugh just as hard. How I do love you, indeed. I'm not afraid to say it. And right now, I'm just barely drunk.

You guys all rock, and make me feel like I have a million dearest friends.

Special thanks to Christina Antus, who saved my big fat ass on technical part of the cover design. Much love and appreciation!!

Thank you.

xoxoxo, Laurie

Made in the USA
Lexington, KY
10 May 2018